# THE SECRETS

## OF

# Angel
# healing

**ALWAYS REMEMBER HOW MUCH
YOU ARE APPRECIATED AND LOVED!!**
*Please share this message with everyone you meet.
Thank you.*

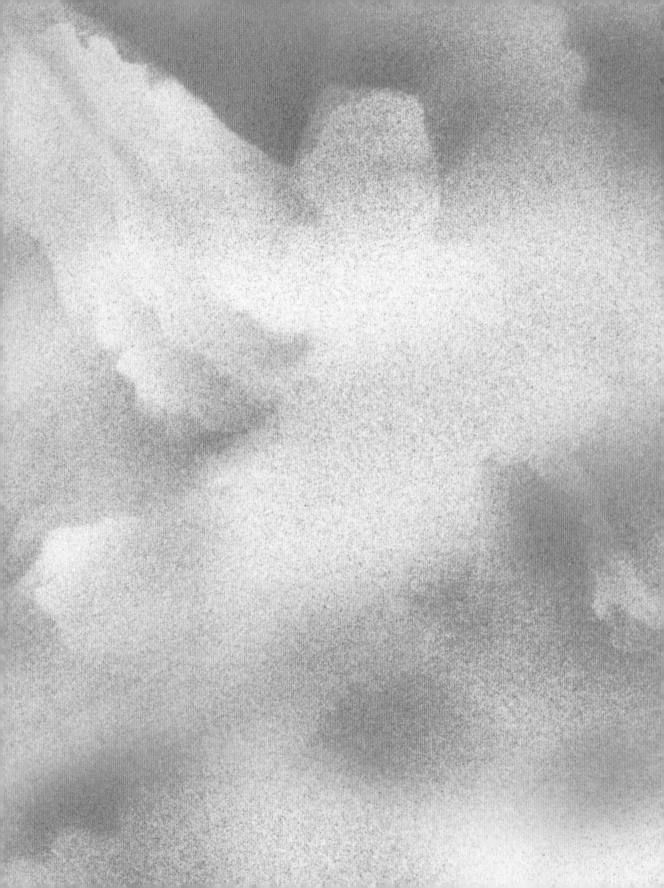

# THE SECRETS OF

## OF

# Angel healing

## THERAPIES FOR MIND, BODY AND SPIRIT

HAZEL RAVEN

A GODSFIELD BOOK
www.godsfieldpress.com

This book is dedicated to Archangel Raziel

First published in Great Britain in 2006 by Godsfield Press,
a division of Octopus Publishing Group Ltd
2–4 Heron Quays, London E14 4JP

Distributed in the United States and Canada by
Sterling Publishing Co., Inc.
387 Park Avenue South
New York, NY 10016-8810

A CIP catalogue record for this book is available from the
British Library

ISBN-13: 978-1-84181-268-7
ISBN-10: 1-84181-268-4

10 9 8 7 6 5 4 3

Printed and bound in China

# Contents

# Introduction

This inspirational guide to angelic healing presents an array of tried-and-tested practical techniques for asking the angels and Archangels to help you overcome problems of mind, body and spirit. You do not need to believe in the angelic realm to receive its benefits. Moreover, you do not need to be clairvoyant or psychic, live like a hermit or take holy vows in order to experience angels.

Angels are completely dedicated to helping humanity spiritually as well as in practical ways. By following the simple exercises in this book you will create a firm foundation from which to open doorways into the angelic realm – the way of love and light.

Connecting and working with angels has never been easier, and humanity's fascination with them is becoming more and more evident. Angel books, cards, CDs and seminars are everywhere; angels (and especially guardian angels) feature on television, in magazines and newspapers, as well as in music and films.

Perhaps angels are more evident today because people are awakening from the spell of materialism, greed and separation from God that was cast by our 'little egos' – our sense of our own importance. Or perhaps God is sending more and more angels to Earth to help with the Earth's spiritual evolution as we approach the 'end of days' prophesied in the Bible as well as by many ancient cultures.

In astrological terms, we are currently making the transition from the Age of Pisces – a time of paternal influence in which we hand over to others responsibility for our own behaviour, evolution and spiritual growth – to the Age of Aquarius, in which we personally take on this responsibility. Working with angels offers everyone the unique opportunity to develop wisdom, strengthen their self-understanding and overcome obstacles by connecting with their inner light, which is a direct pathway to God.

## HOW THIS BOOK CAN HELP YOU

In the chapters that follow you will learn:

- How to sense the presence of angels and, more importantly, how to interpret the signs that angels frequently use. Understanding these signs will help you develop an increasing sense of the presence of angels, which will benefit you in subtle but perceptible ways.

- Creative ways of using beautiful crystals, gemstones, colour and essential oils in order to attract angelic help, blessings and healing.

- How to create angelic spaces in your home that facilitate communion with the angelic realm. Angels will help you purify your environment and put the 'heart' back into your home by turning your living space into a true sanctuary – a haven that is loving and nurturing for your body, mind and spirit.

- How angels can instantly transform the atmosphere of your home, which can ease family problems, especially after a heated argument or quarrel.

- How to get help from the angels in your everyday life. Angels have the capacity to appear spontaneously at dramatic or important moments in your life, leaving a profound sense of the Divine. However, you can contact them whenever you need inspiration, guidance, healing or help.

- How to assist others, as you gain confidence in your angelic contact. You can become a bridge of light by channelling angelic energies. You only have to ask the angels for help in any situation, remembering that they are awaiting your call. You will soon learn how to direct their assistance towards any task (such as stopping crime or helping to create world peace). When a group of people work together and invoke angelic assistance, miracles become possible. I believe that when the angelic realm and the human realm work together, the power to change the world becomes manifest.

- How to awaken yourself to other dimensions and realities. When you learn to relax and quieten your mind, you will open yourself to the endless mystery that is God.

The reason angels can help you in these profound ways is that they have not followed the same evolutionary path as humans. In fact, angels are a completely different emanation of the expression of

God. Traditionally, it is said that angels were 'born' perfect and were made by God on the second day of creation, with the sole purpose of ministering to his creation. In fact, everything in God's creation is governed by an angel.

However, I take this understanding a step further. I believe that as we align our 'human' will (our 'little ego') with God's perfect will, we evolve spiritually and climb the evolutionary ladder. As we do so, we come closer to God. This process of aligning our energy with the God-force in order to achieve union with God is the real reason for working with angels. In spiritual traditions this path is known as Jacob's ladder or the ladder of light, the Tree of Life, or the path of ascent into cosmic consciousness. I believe that through spiritual evolution we have the capacity to become angels ourselves, to ascend to Heaven and exist evermore in paradise.

## VISITING ARCHANGELIC TEMPLES

To assist you in bridging the gap that exists between human consciousness and God-consciousness, this book will teach you how to visit the Archangels' temples (see page 72) in your dreams and meditations and to receive their advice and spiritual aid. Each Archangel has an etheric temple anchored within the planetary grid. These temples have been used by mystics, initiates and 'masters' since the dawn of human civilization. Each temple has a different function and purpose, which will help you on your evolutionary path.

Each Archangelic temple deals with fundamental questions and problems in your everyday life that may have blocked your spiritual growth. When you visit these temples, you will find meaningful answers to questions such as 'Who am I?', 'Why am I here?' and 'Do I have a soulmate?' Each rung of the ladder can be viewed as an initiation that brings spiritual growth. Each step will help you to develop a firm foundation from which to seek and acquire even higher knowledge.

### TUNING INTO YOUR ANGELIC AWARENESS

I feel incredibly fortunate that I never lost my angelic awareness and have always been attuned to the angelic realm. Babies and young children are normally attuned to angels, but as they grow and become part of the physical world, they often close down their awareness of subtle energies – their angelic awareness. Many angel books tell the stories of people who have had an 'angelic awakening' (usually at a major event in their lives), which leaves them with a profound sense of the Divine and of the presence of angels.

As a qualified therapist and teacher, I have always sought to empower others to take control of their own lives. My students and the people who attend my angel seminars come from many different countries, belief systems and backgrounds. I simply wish to awaken those who contact me, enabling them to become more aware of the subtle realms where angels dwell.

My teaching has proved to me that people who are aware of angels have a different view and experience of the world. They believe, as I do, that we are surrounded by legions of angels. We each have a guardian angel, but can also call on the assistance of millions of other angels. Angels are always at our side, especially when we are helping others. I know my clients and students often describe the angels they have seen or felt around me. I can't count the number of times my clients report feeling the touch of 'extra' unseen hands placed gently upon them during therapy sessions. They also describe seeing large spheres of light and how beautiful the experience was.

One note of caution: if, while working with angelic energies, you feel yourself taken over or controlled by any outside force at any time, stop your connection with this energy. You should always ask for confirmation that the angelic contact is

genuine. You'll learn what to look for in the section on angelic signs in How Angels Can Help You (see pages 30–31).

Finally, keep in mind that angels are not judgemental, and your guardian angel will never leave your side. However, it is only polite to thank the angels after you have received their assistance. Gratitude (counting your blessings), humility and dedication to your spiritual path are the surest ways to raise your vibrational rate, which will in turn attract more angelic helpers into your life. Selfishness is a guaranteed hindrance to heartfelt angelic communication, as is a judgemental attitude towards others.

# Part One
# ANGELS IN YOUR LIFE

# What are angels?

## Angelology

The study of angels, or angelology, is a highly complex field, which differs from book to book, from mystic to mystic and from theologian to theologian. Over the centuries numerous manuscripts and books have been compiled and written, and many exhaustive works on angelic hierarchies and scholarly traditions have appeared. However, though at first these works may appear diverse, they are all remarkably similar. Each views angels as winged messengers mediating between Earth and Heaven.

The word 'angel' is in fact derived from the Greek word *angelos*, which translates as 'messenger'. Angels act as bridges between Heaven and Earth and represent channels between the higher, refined, subtle emanations of God (perfect spirit) and the physical material world.

### THE BIRTH OF THE ANGELS

Angels did not follow the same evolutionary path as humans. They were all born at the same moment: perfect, intelligent, immortal and having free will. The vast majority of them instantly chose to give up their free will, preferring to align themselves eternally with their creator. This was their gift of adoration to the perfection of God. However, a few angels wanted their own power and glory – these are the ones known as 'fallen' angels. Those angels who gave up their free will now serve God and protect humanity from the 'fallen' angels. Everything in God's creation is governed by an angel.

In much religious art angels are depicted as perfect beings with wings, but in reality angels are pure spirit and therefore have no physical form. Each person who encounters the angelic vibration will do so in a form that is appropriate to him or her at that time. One person will sense the presence of angels; another will hear them; another will encounter them in a vision, meditation or dream state; yet another will perceive them as a wonderful aroma. Visual manifestations of angels represent the most profound encounters: they might manifest as a winged being, a spinning mandala (a circular design symbolizing the universe) or a glorious shimmering light. Finally, some people may encounter angels as saviours who rescue them from problematic (and sometimes dangerous) situations, when the angels will appear as ordinary human beings dressed in everyday clothes.

Being genderless beings emanating from pure spirit, angels are androgynous, with their male and female qualities in harmony. However, some people may regard a particular angel or Archangel as male, whereas others will view it as female; still others will perceive it as having a twin flame or a female partner (*archeia*) to balance the male energy. This is a case of the human mind attempting to rationalize the Divine in human terms, by assigning a gender to an angel or Archangel's energy signature. Throughout the centuries Archangels and angels have, in fact, generally been portrayed as male.

Angels constantly surround you, and those people who are aware of them believe that legions of angels stand beside them, just waiting to be summoned. Everyone – irrespective of the belief system they support – can benefit from this pure emanation of the God-force. Working with the angelic realm means that you experience only positive emotions, for angels are capable of transmitting only beneficial attributes and love.

## THE HISTORY OF ANGELS

As we have seen, angels are not allied to any particular religion or belief system and are older than civilization itself. Winged beings are recorded in all mystical traditions. At the core of this approach lies the ancient wisdom that underpins the mystic traditions of the different ages.

It is uncertain exactly where on Earth the angelic tradition began, but the earliest writings of Sumeria, Egypt, Persia and India recognized winged beings or the messengers of the gods. On a Sumerian stele (a stone column) dating from the fourth millennium BCE, a winged being (an inhabitant of the Seven Heavens, see pages 23–24) is depicted pouring 'the water of life' into the king's cup. The teachings of Islam and the Judaeo-Christian tradition also have at their core the ideology of the Seven Heavens.

The Bible mentions angels frequently, but with no detail except in two or three instances. Gabriel and Michael are mentioned by name in the Old Testament.

# Angels and the Kabala

One of the richest sources of angelic lore is the Jewish mystical tradition known as the Kabala. *Kabala* is a Hebrew word meaning to receive inner wisdom by word of mouth, in the oral tradition, and this wisdom was originally passed from master to pupil. There are various spellings of the word Kabala, which correspond to different historical periods and traditions, but essentially they all refer to the same thing.

The Kabala is a body of information, rather than a single manuscript or source, although two early texts were *The Zohar*, or 'Book of Splendour', and *The Sepher Yetzirah*, or 'Book of Formation'. The latter was traditionally credited to Melchizedek, a priest-king of Salem (later Jerusalem), and was believed to have been passed to Abraham, father of the Jewish nation, in a revelation.

For centuries the Kabala has been used by mystics as a way to experience the different aspects of creation and has been assessed by them (either through direct personal experience or through spiritual revelation) as a path, map or route to God. The Kabalist structure of existence shows the different stages through which God brought the original Divine scheme into manifestation. Some Kabalists purport that the Kabala dates back to the time of Adam in the Garden of Eden, but because no one is certain about its origins, it is as vital and unique as you are as an individual.

## THE TREE OF LIFE

The expression 'Tree of Life' was used widely for the first time during the Middle Ages. Kabalist mystics regard it as a manifestation of a core reality underpinning the different elements that represent the structure of existence. Divine energy descends from above and gives rise to ten 'sephiroth' (the singular is 'sephirah'): spheres, vessels, circles or points of light, with each sephirah representing an energy signature. The energy signatures on the Tree must balance each other: so, for example, *Mercy* must be balanced by *Judgement* or it becomes weakness; *Judgement* must be balanced by *Mercy*, or it becomes cruelty.

The Tree of Life can be seen as a map showing the route upwards to God-consciousness (return to paradise). To achieve this, you ascend from the base of the Tree to the top in reverse order through the sephiroth (that is, from ten back to one); alternatively, a more direct (and preferable) route is available via the central pillar of the Tree. Whatever your belief system, you can use the Tree of Life as a template to help you comprehend the different processes by which you can access the Divine in your own life, and thereby arrange your life according to the way in which you perceive the world.

There are ten sephiroth spheres and 22 interlocking paths, giving a total of 32 paths of wisdom in the archetypal world.

Between the ten spheres and the 32 paths lie the 50 gates of inner light. Together, these spheres, paths and gates of light make up the Tree of Life pattern. Each interlocking path is assigned a letter from the Hebrew alphabet, and each sephirah is named according to its function and has an associated Archangel that holds its energy signature.

If you are truly committed to working with the angelic realms and wish to attain greater self-knowledge and wisdom, it is important to develop an understanding of the basic principles of the Kabala. The Archangels channel the energies of God; they act like generals commanding their troops and step down the energies to each of the lower spheres on the Tree of Life. Each Archangel holds a special place in the web of creation and has a specific frequency or attribute, enabling it to act as an arch or gateway into spheres of different energy vibrations.

## THE COSMIC POWER OF SOUND

The Hebrew alphabet consists solely of consonants and is believed to be sacred. Each consonant has a vibration or energy signature, giving it a creative cosmic power. This power can be activated only by the human voice when it provides the vowel sounds through Divine understanding.

Kabalists believe that only prayer that is spoken aloud is effective, releasing the cosmic force of God. This force flows down through the sephiroth of the Tree of Life and then through you, permitting the 'Will of God' to be made manifest on Earth. God is omniscient but gave everyone free will, so he and his angels can assist you only if you actually ask for their help. God gave everyone the free will to undergo both good and bad experiences, which may be perceived as a series of life lessons or soul initiations. These lessons are specific sephiroth on the Tree of Life (stages on the path of ascension), which you can access through the 32 paths of wisdom. Once you have fully integrated the attributes of the sephiroth into your daily life, you step on to the path of ascension – the journey of love – and get closer to the Divine.

## THE ABSOLUTE

'In the beginning God created the heaven and the earth. And the earth was without form, and void; and darkness was upon the face of the deep. And the Spirit of God moved upon the face of the waters. And God said, "Let there be light": and there was light. And God saw the light, that it was good: and God divided the light from the darkness.' (Genesis 1:1–5)

At the top of the Tree of Life, beyond the ten sephiroth, lies the Divine: perfect, pristine and absolute. It generates a sequence of negative existences, which must be experienced in order to reach the point of light. These existences are:

- *Ain* = Void

- *Ain Soph* = Limitless all

- *Ain Soph Aur* = Infinite light

The point of light is without limit or dimension, containing all possibilities: omnipotent and omnipresent. It is everything. In the Kabala it is known as Kether or Crown: it represents the start of the Tree of Life and the point from which all the other sephiroth flow downwards.

In the Kabalistic scheme there are Four Worlds of the Tree of Life:

- *Atziluth* represents the spiritual world.

- *Briah* represents the emotional world.

- *Yetzirah* represents the psychological world.

- *Assiah* represents the physical world.

These worlds also symbolize the elements of fire, water, air and earth.

## THE ARCHANGELS AND THE SEPHIROTH

Those who wish to work with angels and Archangels do not need to follow the Kabala (or indeed any system). However, some people do subscribe to the Kabalistic tradition, and it is interesting to note the associations on the path of ascension to the Divine:

- *Kether* or Crown: the Archangel Metatron (Divine).

- *Chokmah* or Wisdom: the Archangel Raziel (Cosmic Father).

- *Binah* or Understanding: the Archangel Tzaphkiel (Cosmic Mother).

- *Daath* or Knowledge: the Holy Spirit. This is a non-sephirah and the external aspect of Kether. It is viewed by some Kabalists as a place of miracles and arcane powers.

- *Geburah* or Judgement: the Archangel Chamuel.

- *Chesed* or Mercy: the Archangel Zadkiel.

- *Tiphareth* or Beauty: the Archangel Raphael.

- *Hod* or Glory, Majesty: the Archangel Michael or Archangel Jophiel.

- *Netzach* or Victory: the Archangel Haniel.

- *Yesod* or Foundation: the Archangel. Gabriel

- *Malkuth* or Kingdom: the Archangel Sandalphon or Archangel Uriel.

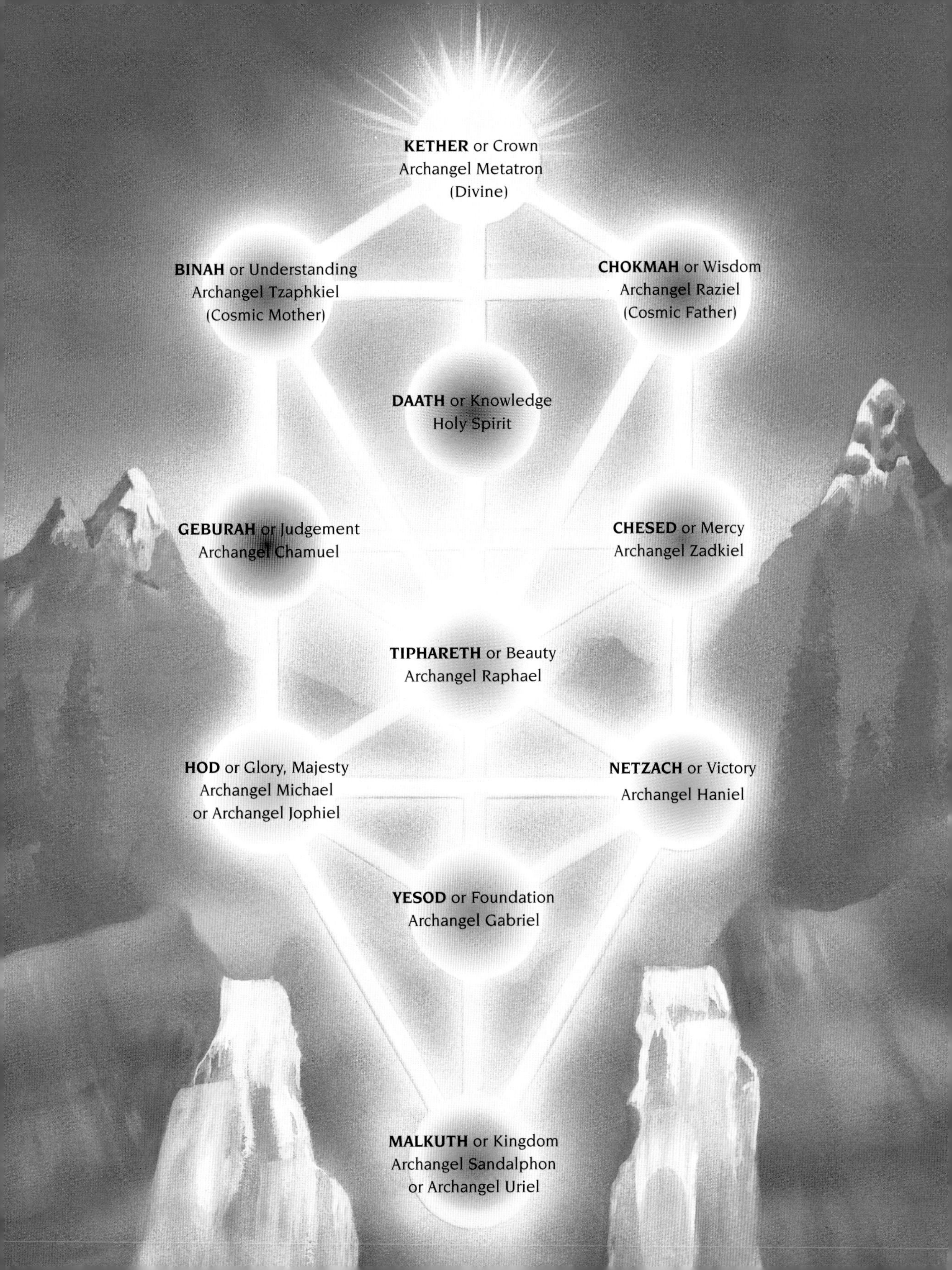

**KETHER** or Crown
Archangel Metatron
(Divine)

**BINAH** or Understanding
Archangel Tzaphkiel
(Cosmic Mother)

**CHOKMAH** or Wisdom
Archangel Raziel
(Cosmic Father)

**DAATH** or Knowledge
Holy Spirit

**GEBURAH** or Judgement
Archangel Chamuel

**CHESED** or Mercy
Archangel Zadkiel

**TIPHARETH** or Beauty
Archangel Raphael

**HOD** or Glory, Majesty
Archangel Michael
or Archangel Jophiel

**NETZACH** or Victory
Archangel Haniel

**YESOD** or Foundation
Archangel Gabriel

**MALKUTH** or Kingdom
Archangel Sandalphon
or Archangel Uriel

# Angel hierarchy

There are three spheres (or levels) of angelic influence from Heaven to Earth, according to the scholar Dionysius. *De Coelesti Hierarchia* ('The Celestial Hierarchies') was supposedly written by St Paul's famous convert, Dionysius the Areopagite, but was actually compiled in the sixth century CE by a Syrian monk, Dionysius the Pseudo-Areopagite. According to this treatise, the Seraphim, Cherubim and Thrones represent the first sphere of influence and are closest to God.

## SPHERE ONE
### SERAPHIM

Seraphim are closest to God and symbolize the highest order of the angels. They are angels of love, light and fire, whose purpose is to inflame the hearts of humans with Divine love and maintain its purity. The word 'Seraphim' means 'the inflamer' and is derived from the Hebrew word *saraph*, meaning 'burning'. Seraphim are therefore the angels of Divine fire. In the Old Testament they place a glowing coal on Isaiah's lips, at which point he is cleansed of all karma (the universal law of cause and effect).

Of their six wings, the Seraphim use two to cover their faces, two to cover their feet and the other two to fly with. They surround the throne of God, singing a hymn of praise known as the *Trisagion*, which translates as 'Holy, Holy, Holy'. Revelation 4:8 states that if you call on the Seraphim's power, you will be flooded with infinite love, light and joy. In medieval symbology they were red and carried fiery swords, while Dante asserted that Seraphim were related to the presence of 'gladness of God'. They specialize in miracles, joy and the path of ascension, and are ruled by the dazzling Archangel Seraphiel (sometimes known as the Prince of Peace) and by Archangel Metatron (who presides over Kether, or Crown, on the Tree of Life).

## CHERUBIM

Next closest to God are the Cherubim, who hold the energy signature of the stars and galaxies and who are also responsible for keeping the celestial records and for imparting knowledge.

Vast cosmic beings, they direct and spread the perfect light of God in the form of love. They are charged with maintaining the purity of God's love, which they radiate outwards into the entire cosmos. However, these mighty Cherubim are not the cupid-like beings often portrayed in art. The word 'Cherubim' means 'fullness of God's knowledge' and is derived from the Assyrian *karibu*, meaning 'one who prays' or 'one who communicates'. Day and night, the Cherubim praise God.

In Assyrian art they are shown as winged creatures with the bodies of eagles, bulls or sphinxes and with human or lion faces. During the Middle Ages. Cherubim were often depicted wearing blue: an apt colour for those who dispense wisdom.

In the Bible they guard the gates of Eden after the fall of Adam and Eve (Satan was one of the Cherubim before he fell from grace). And the Ark of the Covenant had two carved Cherubim, which reputedly gave it awesome power. The Cherubim are ruled by Zophiel, Ophaniel and Rikhiel. In Revelation 4:8, St John refers to them as beasts (holy) Divine beasts with six wings and 'full of eyes within'.

## THRONES

Thrones direct the justice of God, carrying the loving energy further outwards and ensuring that every planet is bathed in God's perfect love. They carry out God's wishes and maintain the purity of the energy vibration. The Virgin Mary is said to be a Throne. Thrones are also referred to as Wheels, because they have a pure, formless energy, resembling huge fiery spheres. In the Kabala they are known as chariots or the Merkavah (see pages 146–147). The Zohar ('Book of Splendour') positions Wheels above Seraphim; others place them as Cherubim. Thrones are ruled by Zaphiel, Zabkiel and Oriphiel.

## SPHERE TWO
### DOMINIONS

Dominions (also known as Dominations) oversee the lower angelic hierarchy. They represent the rule of God over the level where the spiritual and physical realms start to merge, and act as channels for God's love through the energy of mercy. The Dominions' symbols of authority are an orb or sceptre carried in their left hand and a staff of gold in their right hand. They are ruled by Zadkiel and Hashmal.

## VIRTUES

Also called the Lords of Light, the Virtues channel immense Divine light and perform miracles on Earth. Sometimes known as the 'shining' or 'brilliant' ones, they are reputed to inspire the saints, and they give out grace and valour. When he ascended to Heaven Jesus was accompanied by two of this order of angels. They are ruled by Sabrael, Barbiel, Hamaliel and Uzziel.

## POWERS

These are Karmic Lords, who keep the Akashic records (records of all the happenings on Earth, including the deeds of every individual who has ever lived there) and give protection to human souls. Given the task of keeping demons under control, they act to prevent them from overthrowing the world. Powers are frequently viewed as the angels of death and rebirth, and because they guard the pathways to Heaven, they can guide lost souls back on to the right path. They are ruled by Sammael, Camael, Ertosi and Verchiel.

# SPHERE THREE

## PRINCIPALITIES

Principalities guide religions to the path of truth and are in charge of nations, cities and towns, as well as sacred sites. Principalities work with guardian angels to inspire us. They are ruled by Anael, Cerviel and Requel.

## ARCHANGELS

Archangels are heralding angels, who give out God's messages to humanity. Gabriel, Raphael, Uriel and Michael are the best-known Archangels. Each Archangel is described in detail later in this book (see pages 78–157).

## ANGELS

There are literally millions of angels, helping in endless different ways. They guard people and all physical things. They include the angels of Abundance, Balance, Creativity, Courage, Faith, Freedom, Harmony, Hope, Inspiration, Joy, Love, Peace and so on.

### GUARDIAN ANGELS

Everyone has a guardian angel, who can never leave you and who will inspire, comfort and console you throughout your life. Your guardian angel is appointed to you when you first incarnate – it journeys with you through all your incarnations, evolving as you evolve. Some people feel that their guardian angel is actually their higher self or (as Buddhists say) the Divine spark or Buddha-nature within everyone.

### GUIDING ANGELS

Everyone also has a guiding angel, who works with you. Your guiding angel will change as you evolve spiritually or as you need to learn different spiritual lessons, such as self-healing. Some people have several guiding angels working with them at any one time.

## CHILDREN OF THE ANGELS

These are the nature spirits who create abundance and harmony on Earth, where they are appreciated and held sacred. They frequently manifest to humans as dancing coloured lights.

### THE ELEMENTAL KINGDOM

The message of the elemental spirits is 'harmonize with, do not disrupt, nature'. Tampering with nature not only disrupts the harmonious flow of the weather system but also damages the environment. When you work in harmony with the elemental forces, rather than combating them, you create positive energy in your living and working environments. The sense of beauty that we feel in nature is our response to the angelic minds that helped to create it.

### EARTH SPIRITS

Fairies, elves, gnomes and goblins are earth spirits who rule over the trees, plants, flowers, soil, sand and crystals. Earth is the least dynamic and most static of the four basic elements. Earth spirits teach you how to nourish yourself, and how to live responsibly and in harmony with all life on Earth. You can bring stability and abundance to every area of your life by focusing on the powerful energy that flows around you.

### WATER SPIRITS

Mermaids and undines are spirits who rule over the water and tend to the creatures that inhabit this realm. Water spirits teach you to cleanse and balance your emotions, and show you how to go with the flow, by following the path of least resistance. Water can take on any shape: it is often difficult to contain and is sometimes enormously powerful. The water spirits have a lot to teach you about adapting to different situations without losing your fundamental receptivity.

### FIRE SPIRITS

Salamanders are fire spirits (found in significant numbers around volcanoes), who guard the secrets of the transformational fire energy.

Fire spirits teach you about the dynamic energy that lies within you – your life-force. The spark of Divine fire that resides in everyone calls you daily towards the light and awakens you from slumber. Fire burns, destroys and purifies the old, so that something new may emerge, and creative fire can inspire spiritual fortitude.

### AIR SPIRITS

Sylphs are spirits of the air, who convey your prayers to the angels. Air is flexible, free and invisible – it cannot be seen, except by the effects it creates – and most life forms need air in order to survive. Working with sylphs increases your mental prowess, intuition and creative imagination: that sudden flash of inspiration.

### DEVAS

Devas are spirits that have evolved more than the other elementals. They frequently work in association with humans, especially as guardians of ancient groves and sacred sites. They can also be found residing in clear quartz crystals: these devas have the ability to teach you about healing (both of a personal kind and planetary healing).

If you are lucky enough to come across one of these 'devic temple crystals' it will become a tremendous source of information, teaching you how to connect the higher spiritual vibration with matter in order to manifest Heaven here on Earth at this point in time.

# The Seven Heavens

The old saying of 'being in seventh heaven' when you feel deliriously happy probably relates to the New Testament's references to seven ranks of heavenly beings.

The belief that there are Seven Heavens (or seven celestial mansions) is common to the monotheistic traditions of Islam, Christianity and Judaism. The Seventh Heaven, or most refined sphere, is where the perfect essence of God dwells. As we have seen (see page 13), the Seven Heaven tradition goes back some 7,000 years to Sumeria. The Sumerian civilization of Mesopotamia in turn gave birth to the Assyrian, Babylonian and Chaldaean civilizations, which had considerable influence on the religions and angelology of all Near Eastern countries. The names of the Seven Heavens are present in the Old Testament and were given by Enoch as he passed through them on his ascent to Heaven. They are spiritual realms, rather than the astronomical crystal heavens described by Ptolemy in the 2nd century CE.

### THE FIRST HEAVEN: VILON

The word comes from the Latin *velum*, meaning veil and is not a biblical word. This heaven is sometimes known as *Shamajim* or *Shamayim* (a common word for Heaven in the Bible) and is the lowest of the Seven Heavens. It is connected with planetary angels, angels who rule the stars and angels of natural phenomena, such as the atmosphere, wind and water.

### THE SECOND HEAVEN: RAQIA

This is 'expanse' in Genesis 1:6, 1:14 and 1:18. It is ruled by zodiac angels, and some people believe it to be a holding place for sinners awaiting the Day of Judgement. In Islamic tradition it is the abode of John the Baptist. Fallen angels are also held prisoner in the Second Heaven.

### THE THIRD HEAVEN: SHECHAKIM OR SHEHAQIM

This heaven is referred to as the 'skies' in Psalm 18:11. It is a curious heaven, for in its northern regions is Hell: a cold, icy land through which flows a river of flame; here the wicked are punished by the angels, and the land is ruled by the Angel of Death. However, in the southern half lies the Garden of Eden, a paradise, and the Tree of Life, guarded by 300 angels of light. The heavenly garden, with its golden gate, is the realm to which perfected souls go on death; the river of milk and honey and the river of oil and wine run through it. In keeping with sacred lore, Heaven and Hell dwell side by side in the same realm, although this may seem odd to us. St Paul was lifted to the Third Heaven in a vision.

## THE FOURTH HEAVEN: ZEBUL

This is the 'lofty place' in Isaiah 63:15. It is ruled over by the Archangel Michael, and is where the 'heavenly Jerusalem' is situated – the Altar and Temple of God. It is the City of Christ from St Paul's apocalyptic vision. This city was made of gold, with 12 walls surrounding it, another 12 walls inside and 12 gates of great beauty; it was encircled by four rivers: a river of honey, a river of milk, a river of wine and a river of oil.

## THE FIFTH HEAVEN: MAON

This is known as the 'dwelling' in Deuteronomy 26:15. It is the place where God's chosen people sing his praises by day, and the angels sing in praise of God by night. Some of the fallen angels are also held in his heaven.

## THE SIXTH HEAVEN: MAKON

This is the 'habitation' in Psalms 89:14 and 97:2. It is where the Akashic records (see page 20) are stored, together with the details of every individual's punishment or reward (karma).

## THE SEVENTH HEAVEN: ARABOT

This is called the 'clouds' in Psalm 68:5. The highest orders of angels – Seraphim, Cherubim and Thrones – dwell in this abode of God: the Throne, the absolute Holy of Holies. It is the home of unborn souls and blessed spirits.

# Planetary angels

The seven planets that were familiar to the ancients (at least as far back as Roman times) were each attributed to archetypal energetic beings; they were also related to the days of the week over which they were supposed to rule.

The cross-cultural fertilization of Christian, Arab and Jewish heritages in 12th-century Moorish Spain gave rise to the golden age of the Renaissance, representing the end of the Dark Ages. It was also from Spain at this time that the first documentary evidence of planetary angels emerged. From the 16th century onwards this knowledge was suppressed by Puritanism in Europe, but the synthesis of astrology, religion, mysticism and alchemical magic has now resurfaced.

Below are listed the planets, days, virtues and corresponding gemstones associated with particular Archangels, to enable you to petition the planetary angel of your choice. For example, if you wish to bring courage into your life, you would petition Archangel Camael on a Tuesday night and wear a carnelian pendant around your neck.

## ARCHANGELS AND PLANETARY ASSOCIATIONS

| Archangel | Planet | Day | Virtue | Gemstone |
|-----------|--------|-----|--------|----------|
| Archangel Michael | Sun | Sunday | Vitality | Ruby |
| Archangel Gabriel | Moon | Monday | Nurturing | Moonstone |
| Archangel Camael | Mars | Tuesday | Courage | Carnelian |
| Archangel Raphael | Mercury | Wednesday | Communication | Emerald |
| Archangel Zadkiel | Jupiter | Thursday | Abundance | Citrine |
| Archangel Hagiel | Venus | Friday | Love | Rose quartz |
| Archangel Cassiel | Saturn | Saturday | Wisdom | Lapis |

# How angels can help you

## Are angels real?

One of the questions I am frequently asked is how to tell the difference between visualization/imagination and actually seeing an angel. The answer is simple: if you can control or manipulate the image, then it is your imagination. True angelic encounters cannot be manipulated by your conscious mind and have an otherworldly, dreamlike quality about them – although, oddly enough, most people can recall an angelic encounter in great detail, even if it happened many years ago.

### AN ACT OF FAITH

Believing in God, or his angelic messengers, is an act of faith. No one can prove the existence of God or of angels (or even of emotions such as love). All spiritual experiences are subjective; they cannot be quantified, labelled or repeated to conform to the Newtonian laws of physics.

Angels are beings formed from subtle energy. To appreciate this concept, you

need to get to grips with quantum physics, which deals with energy that has no conventional mass. Just because most people are not aware of subtle energy and there are as yet no instruments to measure it accurately, does not mean that it doesn't exist. Imagine trying to explain televisions, microwaves or gamma-rays to your ancestors! Anecdotal evidence regarding the existence of angels will not stand up under scientific scrutiny, but why should it? Angels concern what are perceived as the spiritual realms. They use subtle-energy (the realm of the soul); they speak directly to you through poetry, art, music, visions and deep personal insights. They awaken you through coincidences and subtle impressions. If you become overly concerned with using pseudo-scientific terms in trying to justify or describe the existence of angels and subtle energy, you will lose the Divine experience of the encounter. The invisible realm of the angels is beyond the ordinary mind.

# HELP FROM THE ANGELS

Although angels exist on a different vibratory frequency from humans and you may not necessarily be aware of them, they will respond to your call – normally in answer to heartfelt prayers to God. Angels are God's celestial messengers: they are not your servants, but God's servants.

God sends his angelic messengers to help you through your difficulties. This does not mean that angels will solve all your problems, but they will comfort, inspire and guide you. Remember that angels can never interfere with your free will. So if you want to solve a problem or difficulty in a way that is not for your greater good, the angels will not be able to help you. A lot of people cling to situations and relationships that are dysfunctional, but angels cannot support negativity in any form. However, if you are willing to change and are looking for opportunities to grow spiritually, angels will support you every step of the way and will help to bring better things into your life.

If your life is in immediate danger and it is not your time to die, then God will send his angels to save you. At one seminar a young man shared his own experience. He was riding his bicycle home late one dark and stormy night. The road was narrow, the visibility was poor, and the street lights were obscured by trees, when suddenly a large lorry was bearing down on him. At that moment he knew his life was in serious danger. He closed his eyes and prayed to God, and in that split second he was saved. When he opened his eyes, the lorry had gone past him and he was unharmed.

Another man shared his angel story. He was riding his motorcycle home from work when he came across a large diesel spillage on the road. He skidded, fell off his bike and went sliding down the road, followed by a large truck with its wheels locked in the diesel fuel. The man looked up and could see the truck gaining on him; when he finally came to a stop, the truck was still sliding towards him. When it eventually stopped, his head was under the engine compartment between the two front wheels – amazingly, he was completely unharmed. The truck driver was in a state of shock, though, as he thought he was going to kill the motorcyclist.

When working with angels, you must always work with the energy of trust and positive intent. As long as what you are asking the angels to do is beneficial and will not interfere with other people's free will (or your own life plan), then they will be able to answer your call. It is not appropriate to pray to or worship angels (although you can ask them questions); you simply need to ask God for their help or (to use a more ancient term) 'invoke' them through the power of God.

# ANGELS IN EVERYDAY LIFE

You may wish to develop spiritual insight or to access your inner guidance; or it may perhaps be that you want to develop your healing or creative abilities or need some help in developing successful relationships.

There is no doubt that angels will help you to look at your life in new ways, but it is often difficult getting started. First, try seeking the help of one of these angels in a prosaic, everyday situation and see how you get on.

## ANGELS OF LOVE

These angels are directed by the Archangel Chamuel and specialize in making your daily life more harmonious. There is no task too small or too large for them – they will help in any situation that requires heartfelt communication.

## PARKING-SPACE ANGEL

As you set out on your journey, ask this angel to help you find a safe parking space when you arrive at your destination.

## KITCHEN ANGELS

By asking the angels to assist you in all your positive endeavours, you may find that they turn up in the most unexpected places. Ask the angel Isda to bless your food, making it more nutritious and delicious.

## ANGELS OF LOST OBJECTS

Losing your keys, jewellery or important documents can be very stressful. When this happens, immediately ask the angel Rochel to assist you in finding the lost object.

## TRAVELLING ANGELS

These angels are directed by the Archangel Michael and offer you protection from physical dangers.

## EXAM ANGELS

Ask the Archangel Jophiel and the angels of illumination to help you study and pass your exams. They will also help you to absorb new skills and will offer illumination and wisdom to fuel your creativity.

# Sensing the presence of angels

As people become increasingly aware of angels, so the veil between our world and theirs becomes thinner. You do not need to be clairvoyant or psychic to experience the joy and delight of angelic contact. Some people who never actually see an angel are nevertheless aware of their angel's presence.

Angelic 'calling cards' are personal to you. As you gain experience, you'll learn to recognize your own signs. Here are some ways in which you may become aware of the presence of angels:

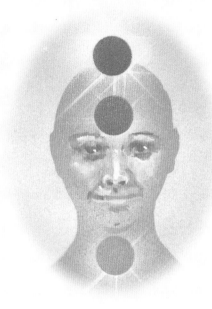

- The atmosphere of the room may change – you may feel surrounded by a warm glow.

- The air may seem to be tingling around you, or you may feel a rush of energy down your spine.

- A beautiful aroma may suddenly fill the room. The rich smell of chocolate is a calling card of some guardian angels!

- You may experience feelings of love or an overwhelming sense of deep peace or of protection.

- Coloured lights may appear from nowhere: shafts of brilliant light, or even spheres of colour, may dance in front of you, especially when you are working with the healing angels.

- During angelic meditation sessions you may experience a bright light in front of you, even when your eyes are closed.

- You may feel the presence of wings brushing against you or enfolding you, or even angelic hands on your shoulders.

- You may become aware of an increase in the number of coincidences that occur in your life. Or your problems may seem to solve themselves – sometimes in the most unexpected ways.

# ANGELIC SIGNS

Sometimes angels manifest their presence in ways that anyone can see. You can ask for an angel to appear as proof of your angelic contact. Here are a few common angel signs.

## CLOUDS

You may see angels in cloud formations, especially over sacred sites or when you have asked for angelic assistance. Sometimes you will notice clouds that resemble feathers.

## FLOWERS

Many people find that their flowers last longer when placed on their angel altar. One student of angel lore found that her roses lasted for months, and, after an especially profound encounter, one of the roses changed colour.

## FEATHERS

White feathers may appear in the most unlikely places. When you have found a white feather, carry it round with you to keep your angel close. Once, when I was teaching an angel seminar, I mentioned that white feathers are a common angel sign. After the seminar a woman said that, despite what she had heard, she was not convinced of the existence of angels. At that very moment another student noticed a pure white feather stuck to the sleeve of her cardigan.

## WORDS

Often, if you have asked for angelic help, you will hear the word 'angel' mentioned in a song on the radio or on television, or someone will say the word to you in an unlikely context.

## CRYSTALS

Angels may suddenly appear in your crystals. They frequently manifest in 'angelic' crystals, such as celestite, seraphinite or angelite, although a form can also appear in clear quartz crystal after you start reaching out to the angelic realm.

# Angel cards

Angel cards are an excellent and popular way of communicating with the angels, and you can purchase packs of cards from any shop that specializes in New Age, holistic or metaphysical items. Angel cards are designed to encourage individual creativity and enhance your ability to interact successfully in relationships. They provide keywords that help you focus on a particular aspect of your inner life, which in turn evokes your intuitive abilities and renews your spiritual connection. However, to enhance the experience of communicating with the angels, it is much more effective to make your own cards.

## MAKE SOME ANGEL CARDS

As you begin to explore your connection to the angelic realm, making your own cards is a great way to enhance your intuition. It is not difficult to fashion a set of cards and you do not need to be artistic.

### YOU WILL NEED

- Some card that is white on one side and coloured on the other
- A pen
- Small, shiny angel shapes to stick on to the cards to 'dedicate' them to the angelic energies (optional)
- A beautiful pouch or box to keep your angel cards in when they are not in use (optional)

### WHAT TO DO

1 On the white side of the card, write down an inspirational quality that you wish to bring into your life – this is called a keyword. There is no definitive list of positive qualities that are associated with angels, so you can make as many cards as you like; you can also add to your cards as you develop your angelic understanding. The 70 angelic qualities that I use, for myself and the groups of people with whom I work, are listed in the box opposite.

2 Once you have finished, place your angel cards in a beautiful box or pouch for safekeeping.

## ANGELIC QUALITIES

| | |
|---|---|
| Abundance | Inspiration |
| Acceptance | Integrity |
| Adventure | Intuition |
| Balance | Joy |
| Beauty | Light |
| Birth | Love |
| Blessing | Obedience |
| Charity | Oneness |
| Clarity | Openness |
| Commitment | Patience |
| Communication | Peace |
| Compassion | Play |
| Confidence | Power |
| Courage | Purification |
| Creativity | Purpose |
| Delight | Release |
| Education | Reliability |
| Efficiency | Responsibility |
| Empathy | Romance |
| Enthusiasm | Sensitivity |
| Expectancy | Serenity |
| Faith | Simplicity |
| Flexibility | Sincerity |
| Forgiveness | Spontaneity |
| Freedom | Strength |
| Friendship | Study |
| Generosity | Surrender |
| Grace | Synchronicity |
| Growth | Synthesis |
| Harmony | Tenderness |
| Healing | Transformation |
| Honesty | Trust |
| Hope | Truth |
| Humour | Understanding |
| Imagination | Willingness |

# INTUITIVELY CHOOSE AN ANGEL CARD

Try one of the following methods to select your angel card.

- Simply pick a card at the beginning of each day. Spend a few moments focusing on the day ahead and see which card attracts your attention. Keep your angel card with you or place it where it is clearly visible throughout the day.

- Choose a card just before you go to sleep, slip it under your pillow and let the angel inspire you while you are in your dream state.

- Pick a card at the beginning of any new project, venture or cycle.

- At New Year select 12 cards – one for each month – and make a note of each card on your calendar.

- Choose a card on your birthday or anniversary.

- Select an angel card for a friend who is absent but who needs your help. Focus on your friend, thinking about his or her problem (healing, a job interview, exams and so on) and see him or her surrounded by the angelic quality of the card you have intuitively chosen.

- At the start of a group gathering, get each participant to choose a card intuitively.

## BODY, MIND AND SPIRIT SELECTION

This three-card spread lets you explore the experience of becoming an integrated, balanced being by working on your body, mind and spirit at the same time, bringing harmony on all levels.

### YOU WILL NEED

- A white candle
- Matches or a lighter
- Angel cards

### WHAT TO DO

1 Choose a time and place where you will not be disturbed. Light your candle and dim the lights. Sit down on the floor.

2 Shuffle the angel cards and spread them out – word side down – in front of you.

3 Close your eyes and clarify your thoughts. Allow your body to relax, by focusing on your breathing.

4 When you feel ready, open your eyes and select three cards. The first card represents your physical body, the second card your mind, and the third card your spirit.

5 Read the words on the cards. Take a few minutes to reflect on each card that you have chosen. How does the first angel-card keyword reflect on your physical body? Do the same with the cards for your mind and spirit. What do these words mean to you?

6 Welcome the presence of the angels into your life. Reflect for a moment, allowing any thoughts or feelings to come into your mind. Let your connection with your angels deepen throughout the following days and weeks. Be ready to make any changes or adjustments that you feel are necessary in your life. This might include breaking old habits, reviewing your relationships or making time for your spiritual side to develop.

7 Ask your angels to give you an insightful dream. This frequently deepens your understanding of the angel quality held by the cards.

8 Look up the angel-card keywords in a dictionary – often the root or origin of the words can give you some valuable insights.

9 When you feel intuitively ready to select another three angel cards, begin by acknowledging the help, inspiration and understanding you have received from your current angel cards. Release your angels with love and gratitude. Then use the same procedure to select new cards.

## TIMELINE: PAST, PRESENT AND FUTURE

This three-card spread helps you to clarify recent challenges, situations or events and know how to act in the present and immediate future.

### YOU WILL NEED

- A white candle
- Matches or a lighter
- Angel cards

### WHAT TO DO

1 Follow the same process as described opposite (see 'Body, mind and spirit selection'), choosing a time and place where you will not be disturbed, lighting your candle, then shuffling and focusing on your angel cards.

2 Close your eyes and clarify your thoughts. Allow your body to relax, by focusing on your breathing.

3 When you feel ready, open your eyes and select three cards: these represent your past, present and future.

4 Place the cards in the following order: the first card on the left-hand side (representing your recent past); the second card in the middle (representing your present situation); the third card on the right-hand side (representing your immediate future).

5 Read the words on the cards. Take a few minutes to reflect on each card that you have chosen. For instance, you might have been ill recently and are asking the angels to help you understand what has contributed to your illness. If you select cards with the words 'Play' – 'Joy' – 'Freedom' you might interpret them as follows: recently you have taken on too many responsibilities, which has caused you to overstretch yourself and given you no time to play (relaxation time), which has caused you to lose your joy for life. You now need to free yourself from some of your commitments in order to bring about healing.

6 End your reading in the same way as usual.

## Peaceful thoughts

The first and most important step in making a strong connection with the angelic realm is to purify yourself and your environment. Angels exist at a higher vibrational frequency than most humans are even aware of, because they live in the world of spirit (subtle energy) while humans exist in the physical world. Angels are naturally attracted to people who have a harmonious higher state of consciousness and who live in a peaceful, relaxed environment that allows them to open their hearts to the angelic realm. So if your mind is full of anger and aggression, you need to purify your mind. Try one of the following approaches to encourage peaceful thoughts and purification.

### WRITE TO THE ANGELS

Whenever you have a problem, you can write a letter to the angels. Open your heart to them: do not hold anything back; simply let your feelings pour through you and on to the paper. Really let go and ask the angels to resolve the problem for your highest good and for the good of all. Then leave it up to the angels. Do not try and manipulate the situation. You may be surprised how quickly your problem is resolved – and very often not in the way you expected. This is because the angels do not have a limited human mindset and can work in ways that humans would not even dream of.

### PURIFY YOUR THOUGHTS

Alternatively, simply write down all your problems: everything that makes you angry or that causes you to behave in an unangelic way. Do not hold anything back; just keep writing, telling the angels about whatever makes you fearful, disillusioned or disappointed. Try not to relive negative events, because this can intensify your emotions – just write them down. When you have finished, do not reread what you have written, but burn the piece of paper. As you do so, feel the cleansing effect this has on your mind.

It is also effective to write to someone who has upset you or caused you pain. You are going to burn the letter rather than send it, so don't hold anything back. As you write to the person, tell them exactly how you feel. Initially anger prepares the body to correct injustice, but it must be released or it solidifies into hatred. You must honour your emotions, but you also need to elevate your consciousness – a wilful act of personal empowerment. When you forgive, you rescind your expectations and your conditions for loving; you forgive for your own sake, but your forgiveness will also affect those you have not been able to forgive. If you persist in holding on to anger, hatred, resentment and bitterness, it gives those people power over you, and eventually these negative emotions will make you ill.

Sometimes you may refuse to forgive, in order to punish someone. A simple way of releasing anger towards them is first to acknowledge what you truly feel about their behaviour, then consciously choose not to punish yourself for carrying this feeling. You can say out loud: 'I now intend to let go and release all my suffering over this situation.' Then visualize the person you need to forgive standing before you: tell

them what you would have preferred to happen and choose to release your expectations. Tell them you now want to be free: they are accountable for their own actions, good or bad. Unite your consciousness with your higher self and your guardian angel – imagine and experience the light, compassion and love flowing into you. Experience unconditional love for yourself. As this feeling builds within you, send this love out to the true self of the other person and say: 'I send this love to you, just as you are and have been. I have no expectations regarding your behaviour, past, present or future.' When you feel at peace with the situation, you are ready to release your anger. Until then, you are bound in karmic chains of hatred and will be linked to this person or situation for eternity. Only forgiveness enables you to become free from the impressions and influences of others.

# Create harmonious space

Everything in the manifest universe is made of energy vibrating at different speeds. To make room in your life for angels you need to clear your home of all clutter and raise its vibration to a higher level.

## CLEAR OUT CLUTTER

- Get rid of your unwanted possessions, giving them to charity or recycling them.

- Clean and freshen your home on all levels (even redecorate, if necessary).

- Check all areas of your home for any objects that are less than uplifting. Old furniture and especially second-hand jewellery needs extra cleansing, so use incense or a smudge stick and let the smoke carry away unwanted vibrations. Remember to leave a window open as an exit route for stale energy.

- Discard clothing you have not worn in the last two years, especially any that no longer fits you or looks drab. If you buy second-hand or vintage clothes, always have them thoroughly cleaned before you wear them.

## CLEANSE AND PURIFY YOUR HOME

- Open your windows daily to let out stale energy – it will be rendered harmless by natural daylight.

- Cleanse your home by using the smoke from incense sticks or sage bundles (this is known as 'smudging').

- Use sound to break up stagnant energy: for instance, a crystal singing bowl, bells, gongs, ting-shaws (small Tibetan cymbals), a rattle or drum. Simply allow your chosen sound to 'wash' through the space. If you are lucky enough to have a crystal singing bowl, use it often to cleanse your home, by tapping it gently with its 'striker' or by moving the striker round the edge of the bowl to produce a harmonious sound. Clapping your hands together is another effective way of breaking up stagnant energy, especially in the corners of a room.

- Use the power of your voice to purify your home. Chanting mantras such as 'Om Mani Padme Hum' creates what the British researcher Rupert Sheldrake calls 'morphic' fields. These fields create shape and form and, if used with focused intent, bring forth the energy of the being

to which the mantra is dedicated. 'Om Mani Padme Hum' is an invocation to Avalokiteshvara, the Bodhisattva of compassion. I often use the simple but powerful 'invocation to the Archangels' at the start of my angel seminars: you just call in each Archangel in turn, starting with the Archangel Sandalphon and finishing with the Archangel Metatron. Or you can call in the Archangels of the four directions: Raphael, Gabriel, Uriel and Michael.

## RAISE VIBRATIONS

- Play 'angelic' music to raise the vibration of your home. There is a lot of New Age music that has been specially composed to tune into the angelic realm. Classical music is also wonderful for lifting the energy of a space.

- Spend some time each day in natural light. It is recommended that people experience 20 minutes each day of direct light. Take off your glasses or leave out your contact lenses while you absorb it.

- Use colour to raise the vibration of your home. Selecting the right colours in everyday items can enhance your well-being. Dark, drab colours drag your energy down, leaving you feeling lifeless and dull. For more information on colour, see pages 46–50.

- Hang Austrian glass crystals in almost any area of the home to bring in the energy of 'refreshing light'. Hanging crystals strengthens your intuition, for they have the ability to break up stagnant areas by sending out myriad prisms of

## THE PATH OF GROWTH

As part of the process of transforming yourself, you need to integrate yourself with your surroundings and with those around you whose life you affect. Your partner, children, family, friends and work colleagues may not always feel comfortable with the 'new' you, since it may mean that they need to change too. It is therefore important to be self-reliant during your spiritual transformation, because other people may regard you as selfish. Look for support from those who will encourage your spiritual growth. Of course, you will get a great deal of help from the angelic realms, but you must remember to ask for assistance, because the angels will not interfere with your own free will.

light, which dapple the room and fill it with the moving energy of the sun. Hang a spherical crystal in a window to raise your spirits: simply by lifting your head to look at the crystal on a regular basis you will boost your energy, sit up straighter and breathe more deeply, making it more difficult for you to remain depressed. Crystals are mentioned in the Bible, and they have been used since the dawn of time to attract wisdom, beauty and healing. For information on using crystals to attract angelic help, see pages 54–57.

- Use essential oils as a powerful way of raising your consciousness, making you more receptive to the angelic realm. For more information on using essential oils to attract angelic help, see pages 51–53.

- Avoid people and places that drag your energy down. You may lose a few friends, but you will soon acquire new ones with a similar vibration to your own. If you persist in surrounding yourself with people who drain your energy, try spending less time with them. Once you hold a higher angelic vibration, you will be able to help others and raise their vibration simply by your presence.

# Keep an angel or dream journal

Meditation attracts angels into your life and can increase your intuition. However, personal angelic experiences, meditation revelations and dreams can dissipate unless they are recorded. After each occasion, give yourself time to assimilate your experiences. Write them down or draw them, however fragmented or nebulous they may appear to be.

## YOUR ANGEL JOURNAL

Choose a hard-backed notebook that you find beautiful (you could customize a plain notebook with angel images). This will become your angel journal. It will represent your magical journey: it will be unique to you and will bring even more angelic energy into your life. The more you open your heart to the angelic realms, the more the angelic realms will be attracted to you.

If you are a pictorial person, you may decide to draw images of your experiences; if you are more verbal, you may want to record them in writing. Don't worry about spelling or your writing style – give yourself complete literary freedom in your journal.

Enter fully into the experience with all your faculties. How did the meditation make you feel? What was the most striking feature of the session? Record your responses in the way that comes most naturally to you.

Don't worry if you can't fully comprehend the experience right away. Subsequent meditations with the same Archangel or angel may refer to

it again. Some experiences will make no sense for weeks, months or even years, so your journal becomes a special way of assimilating your knowledge over time.

## DREAMING WITH ANGELS

Invite the angels into your dreams each night. As you place your head on your pillow, ask the angels to assist you with your problems. Keep a dream journal by the side of your bed and record your dreams as soon as you wake, just as you recorded your meditation experiences.

# Make an angel altar or sanctuary

As an angel aspirant, you need to establish a strong connection with the angelic realms. An angel altar is something tangible to focus on and represents your own personal sacred space – somewhere you can hold an angelic celebration. You can come to your altar each day to seek renewal at this sanctuary charged with angelic energy. You can also create an angel sanctuary outdoors – in fact, it can be almost anywhere.

## CREATE AN ANGEL ALTAR

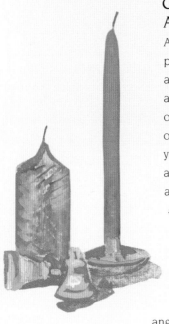

Angels are attracted to places of joy, harmony, love and peace. Making an angelic altar (whatever its size, large or small) also offers you the opportunity to express yourself emotionally, artistically and spiritually, and symbolizes valuable grounding in your transformational work.

It can be helpful to meditate on what you might like to include on your altar, letting your angels guide you. Selecting items inspired by the angels through meditation and visualization will assist your awareness of the issues and challenges concerning the particular aspect of your life on which you are currently working.

Consider including some of the following items on your altar: crystals (see pages 54–57), angelic art, religious icons, angel cards (see pages 32–35), affirmation cards, photographs of loved ones, shells, bells, incense, candles, flowers, essential oils (see pages 51–53), wind-chimes, feathers, a small notebook and a pencil. If you use candles, make sure the room is well ventilated, because they consume oxygen and can lead to headaches or drowsiness. It is important to make sure that your candles are never left unattended while they are burning.

Experiment with the layout of your altar: if a particular item seems out of place or is less than inspiring, remove it. Remember: this is your sacred space and you should only include items that have a specific relevance to you.

Don't forget to include a representation of anything you want to bring into your life, such as love, compassion, spiritual wisdom or abundance.

Get into the routine of attending to your angelic altar daily, whether by cleaning, purifying or reorganizing it – change some of your sacred objects or light some candles. By doing this each day, it will be much easier to set aside some time for meditative thought.

Your altar is a dynamic representation of your angelic journey, so allow yourself to incorporate fun items too.

## CREATE AN ANGEL SANCTUARY

Your angelic altar does not have to be indoors. If you prefer, you can easily create an angelic space in your garden, and most garden centres sell simple statues of angels that you could incorporate in an outdoor sanctuary.

There are no limits on where you can set up an angel sanctuary. In 1990, for instance, I decorated my crystal shop with angels, commissioning my daughter (who is a well-known angel artist) to decorate the ceiling and walls with angel images. Everyone who entered the shop said that they experienced a peaceful vibration. Even today I still have angel pictures in every room.

Don't forget that each time you focus on your angelic space – no matter where it is – it acquires more angelic energy and a higher vibration.

# Be an angel yourself

Visualize your angels. Use your imagination: even if you cannot see them, what would they look like if you could? Write down how you think your own guiding angel appears. This exercise liberates your imagination, which in turns frees your intuition.

When you become adept at working with angels, you will simply go into a meditative state, quieten your conscious mind, tune in and be still. If you have a specific question, you will ask your angel, let your mind go blank and wait for an answer. However, when you are first developing this skill, it helps to follow a meditation ritual like the angelic alignment (see pages 63–65). Also, try the everyday advice given below.

• Practise being an angel yourself by acting as though you were already enlightened. Try to help others as often as possible: take up voluntary work, which helps both your community and yourself.

• Learn to curb your anger. Take a deep breath and mentally count to ten before you reply to a hurtful comment or criticism. Responding to negativity with negativity simply draws in more of the same. Make a positive decision to bring love and light to every situation. Remember that you alone decide on the energy that you hold within your body and subtle bodies: no one else can influence you, unless you let them interfere in your life.

- Eat a well-balanced diet, and take plenty of enjoyable exercise.

- Take time each day to enjoy life to the full, and look for the positive in any situation. Use positive affirmations, such as 'I now choose to allow angelic healing to manifest in my life – I am transformed.' Count your blessings; be grateful, be humble and remember that every day is a benediction – use it wisely to bring Heaven a little closer to Earth. Learn to smile more, and fill your home with love and laughter.

- Read angel books – especially ones that contain stories of how other people's lives were transformed by angels.

- Befriend other angels here on the Earthly plane (through the Internet, if you like). Organize angel gatherings or support groups.

- Learn to be spontaneous. This frees your mind and aids your spiritual development.

- Mentally ask your own angels for assistance. Get into the habit of calling on them first in any situation where you need help. If you don't ask, you won't receive. However, on occasions when you are in danger, a guardian angel may have special dispensation from God to intervene and assist you (this often happens if children are in a life-threatening situation).

# Working with angelic energies

## Light and colour

The physical world that we see is simply a reflection of electromagnetic waves, which glance off objects into our eyes and on to the retina, and this enables us to perceive both light and colour.

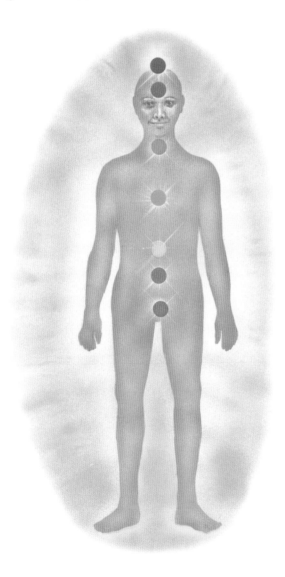

The universe is a magnetic field of positive and negative charges. These resonate constantly to produce electromagnetic waves, each with a distinct wavelength and speed of vibration. These in turn create the electromagnetic spectrum. The radiant energy of pure sunlight is a vital component in nourishing our bodies, minds and spirits. The three primary colours generated by visible light are red, yellow and blue. Every imaginable colour, shade and hue may be created from these primaries, and each colour has its own energetic signature.

There are six main colours in the visible spectrum: red, orange, yellow, green, blue and violet (seven, if indigo is included). Red has the slowest vibration and the longest wavelength that we can perceive; it is warm and stimulating. Violet has the quickest vibration and the shortest wavelength; it is cool and purifying. Green is in the middle; it is harmonizing and balancing.

At either end of the visible light spectrum there are various wavelengths that humans cannot see. Ultraviolet light lies just beyond violet; beyond this there are electromagnetic rays (including X-rays and gamma-rays) with increasing frequencies as the wavelengths get progressively shorter. At the other end of the spectrum, infrared light lies just beyond red light and gives off a more concentrated heat; beyond it there are electromagnetic rays with increasing wavelengths and decreasing frequencies.

Colour surrounds and affects us all, although few people realize how it can be used therapeutically. Light therapy, chromotherapy (colour therapy) and hydrochromatic therapy (colour tinctures) are all ancient methods of natural healing. Nature has given us colour to nourish our whole system, supplying a vital energy that is an essential part of life.

## CHAKRAS AND COLOUR

We respond to colour actively or passively in everything we do. Every minute of our lives (whether we are awake or asleep), light waves are penetrating our energetic system and affecting what we do. Each major visible colour has a particular quality or resonance that is linked to the chakra (energy centre) with which it vibrates. An understanding of the nature of the main chakras and their energetic links to the body is therefore vital in using a particular colour to heal disease or emotional upset, and for spiritual development.

Chakras are funnel-shaped, spinning vortexes of subtle energy. They process this subtle energy and convert it into chemical, hormonal and cellular changes in the body. Each 'master' chakra is also a linkage point associated with specific organs and endocrine glands. Chakras should always be seen as a complete integrated system,

which works holistically. The seven 'master' chakras – Root, Sacral, Solar Plexus, Heart, Throat, Third Eye and Crown – are in line with the centre of the body, with the first five 'embedded' in the spinal column. Each chakra vibrates at a different frequency and is associated with a different element, colour and balance.

- Root Chakra (Muladhara): element of earth; red; balance expressed as grounded, stable and reliable.

- Sacral Chakra (Svadhisthana): element of water; orange; balance expressed as vitality, creativity and originality.

- Solar Plexus Chakra (Manipuraka): element of fire; yellow; balance expressed as logical thought processes, self-confidence and goal manifestation.

- Heart Chakra (Anahata): element of air; green; balance expressed as unconditional love for yourself and others.

- Throat Chakra (Visuddha): element of ether; blue; balance expressed as easy communication with yourself and others on all levels.

- Third Eye (or Brow) Chakra (Ajna): element of avyakta (the primordial cloud of undifferentiated light); indigo; balance expressed as intuition, clairvoyance, clairaudience, clairsentience.

- Crown Chakra (Sahasrara): element of cosmic energy; violet; balance expressed as cosmic consciousness.

# Angels of the rays

Angels of the rays are a particular class of angel, representing the seven rays of spiritual enlightenment. These seven rays are the seven colours of the rainbow and can also be matched to the seven 'master' chakras. Each ray is guided by an Archangel. By invoking one of these energies, you can utilize the full potential of each colour signature, bringing about enormous shifts in awareness and thereby releasing blockages that may have formed in the chakra system.

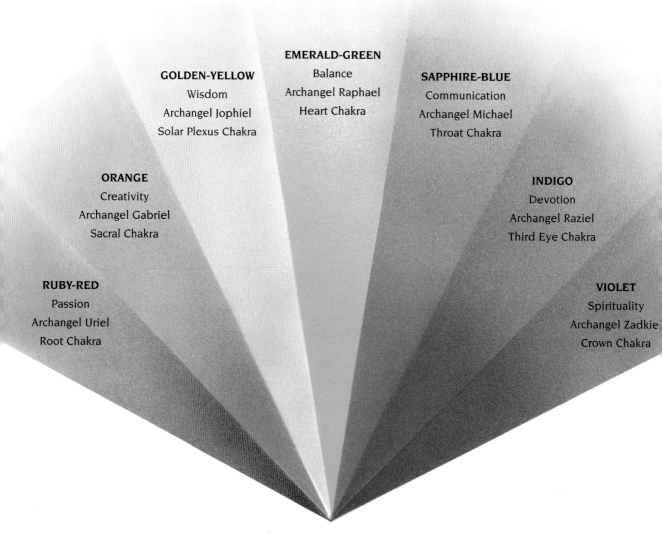

**EMERALD-GREEN**
Balance
Archangel Raphael
Heart Chakra

**GOLDEN-YELLOW**
Wisdom
Archangel Jophiel
Solar Plexus Chakra

**SAPPHIRE-BLUE**
Communication
Archangel Michael
Throat Chakra

**ORANGE**
Creativity
Archangel Gabriel
Sacral Chakra

**INDIGO**
Devotion
Archangel Raziel
Third Eye Chakra

**RUBY-RED**
Passion
Archangel Uriel
Root Chakra

**VIOLET**
Spirituality
Archangel Zadkie
Crown Chakra

## RUBY-RED RAY

Uriel is the Archangel of emotional and mental clarity, who bestows wisdom and inner peace and rescues you from confusion. His name means the 'Fire of God'. He bears a staff as a support and offers unconditional support on all levels. The ruby-red ray teaches you about karma (the universal law of cause and effect) and represents spiritual devotion through selfless service to other people.

*Physical associations*: this ray has the slowest vibration of the spectrum. It releases energy blocks deep within the system, promoting action, the life-force, courage, stamina and endurance, and boosting any processes that have been stagnant. Once survival issues have been resolved, it restores passion and your will to live. It is dynamic and removes fear. It also encourages detoxification by removing inertia, warms the body and increases physical energy.

## ORANGE RAY

Gabriel is the awakening Archangel, who ignites the Divine flame within each person. His name means 'God is my strength', and he aids in the interpretation of dreams and visions. Gabriel is the angel of annunciation, resurrection, vengeance, destruction, mercy, revelation, death and ascension. Bearing a trumpet to awaken your inner angel and bring good tidings, he guides the soul on its journey to paradise.

*Physical associations*: red and yellow are in perfect balance here. This ray ameliorates grief, bereavement and loss, and boosts creativity and optimism. It balances the hormones, promotes fertility and helps to assuage your fears and phobias. A highly motivating ray, it harmonizes the body's energy levels, increases vitality and unlocks deadlocked processes. However, orange works more gently than red does, building up the body's energy step by step.

## GOLDEN-YELLOW RAY

Jophiel is the Archangel of wisdom, who connects you to your higher self, bringing intuition, perception and illumination of the soul. His name means 'Beauty of God'. You can invoke this Archangel whenever your creativity needs a boost or you feel that you have stagnated. He will cleanse, activate and harmonize your mental body, dispersing feelings of low self-esteem and mental confusion.

*Physical associations*: this is the brightest colour of the spectrum. It enhances learning and mental agility, and also tones, stimulates and boosts the body's energy, strengthening weak body processes. It reinforces wisdom, stimulates the intellect and assists concentration. And it enhances feelings of freedom, laughter and joy. This ray cleanses the body of toxins, bringing the sensation of well-being. Finally, it helps to prevent shyness, by stimulating conversationss with other people.

## EMERALD-GREEN RAY

Raphael is the physician of the angelic realm, helping you to heal yourself and find the necessary inspiration to heal other people. His name means 'God has healed' and he bears a cup of healing unguent. His energy is soothing and restorative, although he is also empowered to cast out demons.

*Physical associations*: yellow and blue are totally balanced here, in the ray of great healers and healing, which equalizes, soothes and relaxes. It promotes personal growth by bringing harmony, and keeps your mental and physical energy dynamically balanced. In the body it releases painful tensed-up processes; mentally, it eases feelings of claustrophobia, stabilizes the nervous system, soothes the emotions and reduces mental 'fog'.

## SAPPHIRE-BLUE RAY

Michael is the Archangel who protects humanity, so you can call on him for strength and empowerment. His name means 'Who is as God' and he acts as commander-in-chief of all the Archangels, leading the heavenly forces against demons. His principal colour is yellow and his first domain is the solar plexus; however, because he carries a sword of a blue flame, he is also often connected to the Throat Chakra and the colour blue. The sapphire-blue ray symbolizes the will of God, together with truth, faith and protection.

*Physical associations*: this ray soothes and restrains, calming hot conditions in the body and thereby reducing fevers and regulating hyperactivity and inflammatory conditions. It represents the search for truth and knowledge, encourages communication and brings clarity and serenity. It is useful for the sickroom and for those who are terminally ill; eases ear and throat infections; acts as a natural pain reliever; and lowers high blood pressure.

## INDIGO RAY

Raziel is the Archangel of secret mysteries, who awakens the prophets and religious reformers. His name means 'Secret of God' and he imparts Divine information. He bears the book of wisdom (Kabala). Raziel allows the flames of enlightenment to descend, enabling you to transcend reality.

*Physical associations*: indigo represents the perfect balance of dark blue and dark violet. The strongest painkiller of the rainbow spectrum, it is an astral antiseptic that clears negative thought forms. This ray eases insomnia and sedates the conscious mind, allowing subtle impressions to be registered. It is the domain of psychic understanding, mystery and devotion – the ray of artists and the acting profession. However, indigo can become addictive, and overuse may cause isolation.

## VIOLET RAY

Zadkiel is the Archangel of Divine joy: guardian of the violet flame of forgiveness, transformation, joy and freedom, which transmute lower energies into positive, life-affirming energy. His name means the 'Righteousness of God' and he brings comfort in your hour of need. Zadkiel is also the Archangel of mercy, teaching trust in God and the benevolence of God.

*Physical associations*: violet symbolizes a balance of blue and red: the fastest vibration in the spectrum. It represents a transition between what is visible and invisible to human vision, so it signifies Divine alchemy and the transmutation of energy. It cleanses, purifies and represents spirituality. It is used for past-life regression, psychic protection and to clear karmic debris.

# Angelic essential oils

Essential oils are naturally occurring aromatic substances produced by many different plants, and their beautiful fragrances represent one of the most powerful tools for attracting angelic help. Scent is a subtle etheric form of communication, which heightens consciousness because it carries the essence of a plant. And, by appealing to your sense of smell, plants communicate with you on a deep, instinctive level. Your fragrance receptors are located in the part of your brain that is intuitive and not governed by your logical mind.

Our ancestors were well aware of the etheric qualities of essential oils, which were widely used by priests and priestesses of virtually all religions. Fragrant oils were employed to attract spirits, goddesses and gods, to banish evil spirits and to purify places of worship. Devotees anointed themselves with sacred scents to facilitate divine communication.

Essential oils are volatile, highly concentrated fragrant substances. Store them in a cool, dark place, and avoid evaporation by making sure that the bottle is always tightly closed.

## USING ESSENTIAL OILS

There are many different ways of using essential oils in association with your body, mind and spirit.

- Massage is one of the most common methods used by aromatherapists. It relaxes the physical body, relieving stress and tension. Fragrance works directly on the deepest levels of the emotions, while the therapeutic qualities of the oils are absorbed by the skin. To make a simple massage oil, blend five drops of your chosen essential oil with one tablespoon of a base oil, such as sweet almond or apricot kernel.

- Bathing with essential oils is an ancient method of purification. It stirs up the senses and brings attunement to subtle energies. Blend five drops of your chosen essential oil with one tablespoon of base oil, then add the mixture to a full bath.

- Flower waters may be used to consecrate and cleanse sacred or magical spaces prior to ritual or meditation. You can also anoint sacred objects and candles with them, and they are an old favourite in skincare. Rose, lavender, neroli and jasmine are particularly suited to skincare and are often used as perfumes. Oil is, of course, insoluble in water, but during the infusion process subtle energy and fragrance are transferred to the flower water. Add 30 drops of essential oil to 100 ml (3½ fl oz) of spring water. Leave to infuse for a few days in a cool, dark place, then filter through coffee filter paper before using.

- Anointment is the most ancient and traditional way of using essential oils. Dilute some essential oil, following the recipe given above for baths and massage. Use it as a perfume or for protection, applying it to sacred objects such as candles and crystals.

- A room spray is a heavenly way of using essential oil, as it quickly purifies and sanctifies your sacred space. Add five drops of essential oil to 50 ml (2 fl oz) of pure water in a glass atomizer bottle. Shake the bottle each time you use it to combine the oil and water. Avoid spraying it on polished surfaces.

- You can buy special metal or pottery rings that sit on top of light bulbs in lamps. The rings are hollow in the centre to hold the essential oil. Place the ring on the light, add five drops of essential oil to the ring and switch on the light.

# ARCHANGELIC CONNECTIONS

The choice of essential oils for invoking angelic energies is very much a matter of personal preference. However, the following oils have been used to contact specific Archangels.

- Anise star and lavender to contact Archangel Raphael, for healing of body, mind and spirit. Anise star is used for consecration and offers protection from negative energies. Lavender brings regeneration and heals auric damage.

- Ylang ylang, jasmine and camphor to contact Archangel Gabriel, for inducing optimism, lifting sadness and opening yourself to the angelic realms. Ylang ylang lifts sadness and opens you to the angelic realm, while jasmine induces inner strength and attracts angels. Camphor dispels negative energy, brings purification and can be used to cleanse crystals.

- Frankincense and myrrh to contact Archangel Michael, for empowerment. Frankincense is used for purification, protection, courage, consecration, meditation and for help in overcoming fears and negative feelings. Myrrh is considered one of the holiest essential oils. It is used for purification, dispelling harmful or negative energy, protection and letting go of sorrow or grief.

- Benzoin to contact Archangel Zadkiel, to gain wisdom and understanding. Benzoin promotes detachment and the letting go of painful emotions.

- Rose otto to contact Archangel Chamuel, to open the Heart Chakra. Rose otto is associated with love, inner peace and compassion.

- Neroli to contact Archangel Seraphiel, to clear mental confusion by attracting positive energy and happiness. Neroli soothes fear, worry, restlessness, hysteria and shock.

- Sandalwood to contact Archangel Sandalphon, to bring spiritual awareness, inner peace, alignment with the higher energies and spiritual purpose. Sandalwood dispels negative energies and is used in meditation practice.

- Lemon to contact Archangel Jophiel, to promote clarity of mind, refresh the spirit and break apathy and inertia. Lemon is highly energizing.

- Sage to contact Archangel Metatron, bringing purification and protecting the aura from the forces of darkness. It is also used to gain wisdom and spiritual understanding, and before divination practice. Sage has the power to transform darkness into light.

# Angelic crystals

Since ancient times the properties of different crystals have been used for healing, divination, physical adornment and magic. Humans have always searched for ways to beautify themselves, and carrying protective stones as amulets or wearing them as jewellery are two of the simplest ways to utilize their natural potential. Evidence has been found of the use of gemstones as jewellery as long ago as the Palaeolithic age.

Crystals have a unique aura of mystery, because they never lose their colour, beauty or value, and this aligned them in many ancient civilizations with the spirit world and with Heaven.

## SELECTING CRYSTALS

When you come to select your own crystals, you can look up their healing properties in a book, because all crystals and gemstones are attuned to particular resonances. Alternatively, find a crystal that attracts you. By following your instincts and trusting your intuition, you will begin to trust yourself. You can confirm your selection by dowsing with a pendulum or by passing your hand over the crystal to see if you can feel an energetic connection. The sensations that you will experience as you make a strong connection are:

- An electric-like charge or tingling on your skin or in your hands.

- Heat or cold.

- A pulsing or twitching in your fingers or hand.

- A flush or wave of heat passing through your body.

- Feelings of being enclosed by the crystal energy field.

## CARING FOR YOUR CRYSTALS

To purify your crystal, choose a process that will not damage it. Some crystals (such as talc, halite or selenite) are soft and water-soluble, while celestite and other delicate crystals can separate in water. Placing a crystal in salt water will damage its crystalline structure, making it appear cloudy or change colour; salt will also extract the water from an opal.

Some crystals (such as celestite and kunzite) can lose their colour in strong sunlight. And when crystals of differing hardness are stored together (even when they have been tumbled or polished in a large drum until they are smooth and shiny), they will become damaged – the harder crystals will always scratch the softer ones.

Allowing other people to touch your personal crystals or jewellery will result in their becoming contaminated with foreign emanations, which may not be compatible with your energy field.

## CLEANSING CRYSTALS

It is important to purify your crystals both before and after use. This ensures that any residual disharmonies are removed and that your crystals are filled with positive energy. You can use the following methods to cleanse crystals.

- **Sea salt** Place the crystals in a large bowl of sea salt, then carefully brush off all the salt afterwards. Opals can be placed in a small glass dish embedded in a larger dish of salt.

- **Water** You can use a stream, waterfall, river or spring water. As the water flows over your crystal, hold the intention that all negativity will be washed away and the crystal re-energized.

- **Smudging** This is an excellent form of purification, not only for your crystals, but to prepare yourself and your healing/meditation space. Allow the smoke from your sage bundles to pass around the crystal, removing any residual disharmonies. Remember to keep a window open to give the stagnant energy an escape route.

- **Sound** Using soundwaves to wash through your crystals is an effective way of purifying large quantities – for example, if they all need cleansing at the same time. For this process you need a crystal singing bowl, a bell, ting-shas or a tuning fork (see page 38).

- **Specialist crystal cleansing products** These come in atomizer bottles and can be used to clean all crystals and the environment instantly.

Once you have cleansed your crystals you should dedicate them to the angels. This protects them from negative energy.

## PROGRAMMING CRYSTALS

Only clear quartz crystals are modifiable or 'programmable'. All crystals and gemstones automatically contain their own specific resonance.

To programme a quartz crystal, simply hold it to your Third Eye Chakra and concentrate on the purpose for which you wish to use it. Allow your crystal to fill with this energy. Say aloud: 'I programme this crystal for angelic attunement, healing, love and meditation.' Remain positive when programming your crystal.

## MEDITATION WITH CRYSTALS

In metaphysical circles it is believed that there are certain crystals naturally attuned to the angelic realm (such as those described below). This alignment is often due to their appearance or name. When these crystals are used in meditation or placed on your altar, they will greatly increase angelic awareness by elevating your consciousness.

Hold your chosen 'angelic' crystal in your receiving hand – this is normally your left hand if you are right-handed, but experiment by holding the crystal for several minutes in each hand. Some people prefer to hold a crystal in each hand. There are no set rules, and part of working with the angelic realms involves personal exploration of subtle energy.

### ANGEL-AURA QUARTZ

The shimmering shades of iridescent colours that play within this crystal swiftly attune the senses to the angelic realms of love and light. They purify and uplift your spirit, flooding your energy field with 'sweet' sparkling rainbow bubbles of protection. This crystal transports your awareness to the 'inner temple' of the higher self – where knowledge of your guardian angel is stored. Your guardian angel (see pages 74–77) holds the blueprint not only for this incarnation but also for all your past incarnations, as well as your reason for incarnating in this lifetime. Physically, this crystal is used for purification and for the release of stress.

### ANGELITE

This is a heavenly blue stone, often with the appearance of white angelic wings. Angelite combats fear, bringing inner peace and tranquillity. When used during meditation, it elevates your consciousness to the most heavenly realms of celestial light. It enhances telepathic communication and encourages compassion. When applied to the feet, it will clear the meridians (energy channels) of blockages. Angelite is formed from celestite (see below) that has been compressed over millions of years, and it has many of the same angelic and spiritual properties.

### CELESTITE

This crystal initiates angelic contact, teaching you to journey freely to the celestial realms and find visions and inspiration that will enrich your life. When used with dedication, commitment and love, celestite allows you to discover your soul connection to your guardian angel, and bestows faith in yourself and the confidence to move ahead with grace and ease. This helps you formulate a plan to improve your life by creating a future that is more in tune with your eternal Divine nature. It allows you to reach your highest potential by seeing the greater reality. Celestite stimulates clairvoyant and telepathic communication, dramatically improves dream recall and initiates out-of-body experiences.

### DANBURITE

Danburite is often found with angelic formations within it, which draw enlightenment and spiritual cosmic light. It helps you connect to the communication currents of the angelic domain. Danburite activates the Heart Chakra and integrates it with higher consciousness. The brilliance that this crystal carries is not a colour, but the original light; not an earthly vibration, but cosmic light representing the Divine intelligence. Danburite clears away cloudiness from the aura (the subtle energy field that surrounds the body), adding lustre and beauty. When worn or carried, it gives you a joyful connection to the angelic realms and access to serenity and inner wisdom.

### RUTILE QUARTZ

Also known as 'angel-hair quartz', due to the inclusions of fine golden needles of rutile, this crystal has been used as a talisman since ancient times. It is known as the illuminator of the soul. It clears the pathway for necessary action by exposing flaws and negativity. By sustaining the vital life-force, it restores vibrancy and vitality. It also breaks down barriers, fears and phobias that have held up your spiritual progress. Use rutile quartz to bring about change and for rejuvenation and new directions. It cleanses and balances the aura, filling it with spiritual light and repelling negative energy from both the physical and spiritual worlds.

### SERAPHINITE

This beautiful, deep green gemstone with its feathery, silver iridescent markings activates angelic contact with the highest realms of love, light and especially healing. It is a powerful heart-healing crystal, which also dynamically purifies the 'spiritual' spine. Seraphinite brings balance and stability to the Heart Chakra and aligns it with the Crown Chakra. Its magic makes you feel that it is good to be alive; it helps you to succeed without struggle, by harmonizing the desires of the heart into perfect alignment with your soul's true desire for enlightenment.

### SERIPHOS GREEN QUARTZ

This crystal comes from the beautiful Greek island named after the Seraphim, the highest order of angels. Its delicate pale to deep olive-green crystals bring harmony, balance and emotional stability. Seriphos green quartz is a 'paradise' crystal and swiftly attunes the senses to the healing potential of the angelic realms. It is used for opening, cleansing and activating the heart centre, which allows you to experience love and compassion for yourself and others. This quartz is soothing and comforting to the emotions, which helps to heal a broken heart. It is also an excellent aid for those people who are uncomfortable in their physical body, as it brings them into a constant state of awareness of the higher angelic realms.

# Meditating with angels

## Visualization

Visualization is a form of guided meditation. It is a major spiritual practice or technique, which is used to take the mind away from your everyday concerns and worries. It is often performed in combination with relaxation techniques, which relieve stress, anxiety and tension, enabling your life-force to flow freely. As your body relaxes, so your heart, brain and lungs are slowed down, calming your emotions.

Visualization is the process whereby you internalize your view of the world and, by using specific techniques, alter your outer world (including your health and overall experience of life). Complex visualizations may take time to master but will teach you to focus your mind.

Nearly all visualizations begin by getting you to view something with your mind's eye. Many people are concerned that they will not be able to visualize. Don't worry – everyone can visualize; just think of a time when you were happy. Picture the scene, whether it was a party, a holiday, a wedding or some other event. A mental picture will come into your mind: that is visualization. You may even be able to remember sounds, smells, feelings or emotions. It is not important to achieve cinema-like clarity; simply carrying out a visualization opens the emotional pathways to angelic healing. The more you can clear your mind, the easier relaxation becomes. Mindfulness involves becoming aware of your thinking patterns.

# ANGELIC RELAXATION

When you are undertaking meditation or visualization, it is important that you learn to relax, because this relieves stress, anxiety and tension, letting your life-force flow freely. As your body relaxes, your heart, brain and lungs slow down, calming your emotions.

Relaxation techniques work with the unconscious mind, which contains all your wisdom, memories and intelligence. It is the source of your creativity and connects you directly to your higher self and your guardian angel. Your unconscious mind also regulates body maintenance and autonomic processes, such as breathing, blood circulation and tissue regeneration. The conscious mind does not heal a cut or accelerate your heartbeat to the correct rate; the unconscious mind does that. It is the seat of your emotions and directs nearly all your behaviour.

## WHAT TO DO

1 Sit comfortably in a chair or lie on the floor on a yoga mat.

2 Start by visualizing roots growing from the soles of each foot – extend these roots deep into the earth. This will establish a strong connection to the earth, making you feel safe, secure, balanced and receptive.

3 Begin to relax each part of your body, starting with the feet and legs. Work systematically through your entire body, right up to the top of your head.

4 Release any remaining tension by scanning your body from the top of your head to the tips of your toes. If you feel any tension, tighten the muscles in that area and, as you relax them, breathe out the tension. It is important to take the in-breath through your nostrils, and to exhale through them too – unless you are in pain (physical, mental or emotional), in which case the out-breath can be through your mouth to release the pain or discomfort.

5 Once your body is relaxed, take three slow, deep breaths and ask your unconscious mind to connect you to your higher self and guardian angel.

6 As you breathe in, imagine you are breathing in brilliant white healing light, which is being directed towards you by your guardian angel.

7 With each in-breath, feel your body overflowing with this beautiful light. Notice how calm and relaxed you feel.

8 On completion of the session, you will feel refreshed and alert. Allow yourself plenty of time to come back to everyday waking reality, by becoming aware of your breathing. Feel the weight of your body on the chair or floor. Move your toes and fingers. Allow your eyes to open. Feel how centred and relaxed you are.

# Angelic meditation

We all need a sanctuary for our soul, a space of our own – somewhere we can shut out the world and be entirely ourselves. A dedicated room or area within your home, which you can keep solely for meditation, rituals or contemplation, is best, because it will quickly acquire an ambience of peace, serenity and tranquillity that will recharge your spirit in moments of quiet relaxation.

## MEDITATION POSTURE

Try to sit cross-legged, or in the half-lotus or full lotus yoga posture; these classic forms make a triangular path for the energy field, preventing it from dissipating in all directions. When you sit, face north or east to take advantage of favourable magnetic vibrations.

For long meditations, choose to sit in a comfortable, steady posture with your spine and neck held erect, but not tense. This means that the base of your spine needs to be higher than your knees, thereby tilting your pelvis forward to a position where the spine naturally remains upright when relaxed. The easiest way of doing this is to put a small, firm cushion beneath the base of your spine. The psychic current must be able to flow unimpeded from the base of your spine to the top of your head.

If you are sitting on a chair, choose a straight-backed one to give you support and prevent your diaphragm cramping. Your feet should be flat on the floor, with your hands resting (palms upward) on your knees. Do not let your head loll forward, as this will restrict your breathing.

You can also lie on your back on the floor, and this will give you a different meditation experience – usually sensory ventures into other states are heightened when you are lying down in a sleep posture. These trance-like dream meditations can be very intense. If you choose to lie down, use a yoga mat or rug for comfort. Keep your arms and legs straight but relaxed, and take off your shoes.

## MEDITATION TIPS

- Your room or meditation space should be comfortably warm but well aired, especially if you use candles or incense, which burn up the room's oxygen.

- Keep the room clean and simple: this will heighten your concentration by cutting out distractions.

- Colour is very important. Many people favour the classic simplicity of white, but if you feel more comfortable with colour, then a soothing pale blue or spiritual lavender might be more beneficial to you.

- Choose a regular time to practise your meditation. The most effective times are dawn and dusk.

- Make sure you will not be disturbed for 20–30 minutes.

- A simple angel altar (see pages 42–43) can be a useful spiritual focus; or choose something from nature, such as a beautiful crystal (see pages 54–57).

- Make yourself comfortable. Pillows, cushions, rugs or a cosy chair will add a feeling of comfort.

- Make sure that you are warm: use a blanket to cover yourself, because your body temperature may drop during meditation or visualization.

## PREPARATION

Angels will be very happy to work with you, and often you will feel emotions of excitement and happiness even before you begin the meditation. As you prepare yourself, take note of the following suggestions.

- You may wish to light a candle, choosing an appropriate colour, such as white, pink or purple.

- You can purify your energy space with incense, room sprays (see page 52) or an essential oil diffuser.

- Alternatively, put a drop of essential oil on one of your palms, then gently rub your hands together. Inhaling the fragrance swiftly transports you to an altered state of awareness. Rose otto or neroli is an excellent angelic oil for opening the Heart Chakra, dispelling fears and attracting positive energy.

- Soothing angelic music is also useful, as long as the music does not distract you too much.

- Flowers are very acceptable as energy offerings to the angels. Angels also like the sound of bells. Ringing a small bell at the beginning and end of a meditation is a useful way of acknowledging your sacred time.

- You could also hold a crystal, such as seraphinite, danburite, angelite or celestite (see pages 56–57).

- Purifying your physical body by taking a shower or bath and putting on clean clothes can make you feel more receptive and in tune; after all, you are going to invite angels into your life.

- Wear loose, comfortable clothes. White or pastel colours are best because dark colours drag your energy down.

# ANGELIC ALIGNMENT

This meditation will help you find your angelic guide by putting you in touch with the celestial realm. You may wish to pre-record the following instructions on tape. However, as you gain confidence, you will find you no longer need them but will complete the sequence automatically.

## WHAT TO DO

1 Sit in a comfortable meditation posture (see page 60). If you cannot sit cross-legged, sit on a straight-backed chair with your feet flat on the floor.

2 Put your hands on your thighs (palms upward) and join your thumbs to your index fingers. Now pull your shoulders back slightly and your chin in a little, so that there is a slight pull on the back of your neck, which will ease the blood flow to your brain. Shut your eyes and, with your mouth open slightly, rest the tip of your tongue on the roof of your mouth, just behind your teeth. This positioning is vital, because it maintains the natural flow of energy to your head, while simultaneously keeping your jaw relaxed.

3 There are two main energy channels, or meridians, in the body: the Yin channel (known as the Conception Vessel) begins at the perineum (between the anus and genitals) and flows up the centre of the body at the front, ending at the tip of the tongue; the Yang channel (or Governing Vessel) begins at the perineum and flows up the centre of the body at the back, over the top of the head and back down to the roof of the mouth. These two significant currents are connected when the tongue is touched to the highest point in the roof of the mouth. An easy way to open this channel is to sit in a relaxed pose and let your energy complete the loop, by allowing your mind to flow along with it. Begin in the mouth, and mentally circulate your attention with the flow of energy. Eventually the current will begin to feel warm in some places as it loops around. Relax, trying to bring your mind directly to the part of the loop that is being focused on. Experience the actual flow of energy in that particular part of your body.

4 Once the circuit is working smoothly, inhale as you mentally travel up the spine and over to the Third Eye; exhale as you move down from the Third Eye to the perineum. Complete seven of these circuits. Because it is a mystical number, seven will clear all your master chakras.

5 When you feel ready, bring the energy up your spine as you inhale and send it on up to Heaven. Send with it your gratitude for all the good things in life. As you do so, imagine an overcast day: visualize the clouds parting, as a ray of cosmic white/gold light penetrates and settles directly on your head.

chakra as a beautiful, deep rose-pink colour. Stay with this loving energy for several minutes as you let your Heart Chakra expand.

10 Let the consciousness that transcends normal thought and ordinary senses begin to take you – beyond space and time – into a state of heightened awareness. This is your link with an unlimited realm of angelic understanding and knowing.

11 Now is the moment to make contact with your angelic guidance. From the depths of your Heart Chakra, where your Divine spark dwells, send out your yearning for an angel who will act as a guide in your spiritual development. Feel your longing going out into the angelic realms of love, light, joy, healing and Divine understanding. Request a guiding angel who will be your own particular companion and guide.

12 Feel your guiding angel drawing closer. Experience the transformation as you link into the higher consciousness of the angelic realms. Imagine your angel

6 Absorb this celestial light into your being through the top of your head. This is your link with the Divine source – your connection with everything that ever was, is or ever will be.

7 Let the celestial light pour in through your body. Feel it nurturing every cell, every fibre of your being, with pure consciousness. Relax by allowing any tension or resistance to be released from your body on the out-breath.

8 Bring in the angelic blessings that are meant for you. Feel this positive energy coursing through your body. As you receive Divine benediction, sit with the energy, basking in it. Allow it to bathe your body internally and externally. Notice how calm and relaxed you feel.

9 Now focus awareness on your Heart Chakra. This is where the angels connect with you most strongly. Visualize the

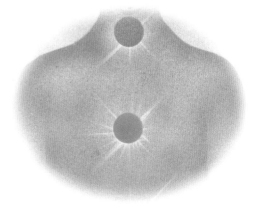

standing beside you and enfolding you in its wings. Feel the unconditional love it is directing towards you. If you are clairvoyant, you may see the most wonderful colours or even a vision of your angel. Be open to any symbols, images or pictures that your angel is showing you. If you are clairaudient (with the ability to hear sounds beyond the range of normal hearing), you may hear angelic music or your angel speaking directly to you. In your 'mind's ear' imagine your name being spoken very gently by the wisest, most compassionate voice. This is your angel speaking directly to your heart. Be aware too of any beautiful aromas, for angels often 'gift' you the fragrance of Heaven.

13 You may wish to ask for guidance or even your angel's name. Keep still and wait patiently for an answer, telling your conscious mind to step aside, if necessary. Breathe deeply and let yourself relax completely. Breathe out all resistance you may have to making angelic contact. Stay in touch with your emotions, for often it is your feelings that will connect you to the angelic realm.

14 When you get an answer, give thanks (make sure you always give thanks). Focus on your gratitude towards the angel that has answered your call and your question(s).

15 It is now time to come back to everyday waking reality. However, before you do so, make an appointment to meet your guiding angel again.

16 Give yourself plenty of time to come back to reality, by becoming aware of your breathing. Feel the weight of your body on the chair or floor. Move your toes and fingers; open your eyes. Connect back with the earth, imagining roots growing out of the soles of your feet, if necessary. Feel how centred and relaxed you are.

17 At the end of the meditation, take a few moments to record your experience. Write down any messages, symbols, thoughts or impressions you received. Do not edit or change the words, but record them exactly as they were given.

18 Keep your appointment to meet your guiding angel. The more you practise this meditation, the stronger your alignment to the heavenly realms will become. Don't worry if you feel very emotional and full of loving energy after connecting with the angelic realm – this is entirely normal.

## COLOUR BREATHING

You can use this simple technique for yourself or for someone else for healing, pain relief, relaxation, balance or as a 'rainbow tonic'. It will determine which colour ray (see pages 48–50) you are most in need of, in order to bring harmony and stability into your life. If you have a need of a particular colour, work with the Archangel who directs that ray. Alternatively, you can simply invoke the 'angel of the ray' of a colour to which you are intuitively drawn.

It is important to take the in-breath through your nostrils, and to exhale through them too – unless you have any condition (physical, mental or emotional) that makes this uncomfortable, in which case the out-breath can be through your mouth. You can use colour breathing to fill your whole body or just part of it, if you have an area of the body that particularly needs healing.

### WHAT TO DO

1 Sit comfortably in a chair, or lie flat on the floor on a yoga mat.

2 Close your eyes and start to breathe deeply, consciously relaxing every part of your body. Begin at your feet and move slowly up your body until you reach the top of your head.

3 Imagine each part of your body getting heavier and heavier. This may take several minutes.

4 Now feel yourself getting lighter and lighter, until you are completely relaxed.

5 In this relaxed state, invoke the Archangel Zadkiel to fill the air around you with the colour violet.

6 Breathe in to a count of three, visualizing yourself inhaling the colour violet as you

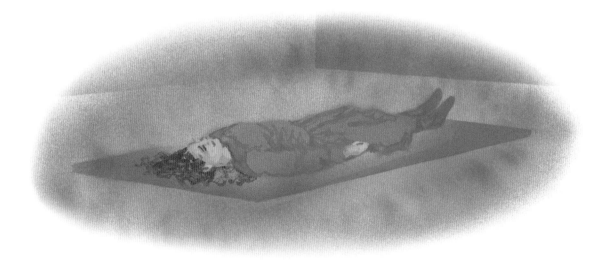

do so – really see yourself pulling the colour in through your nose from the air, then watch it going into your body.

7 Hold your colour breath for a count of three.

8 Now exhale to a count of three.

9 Repeat steps 6, 7 and 8 twice more to complete the first of the three-breath colour cycles.

10 Now invoke the Archangel Raziel to fill the air around you with the colour indigo. Breathe in to a count of three, visualizing yourself inhaling the indigo as you do so – see yourself pulling the colour in through your nose from the air, then watch it going into your body.

11 Hold your colour breath for a count of three.

12 Exhale to a count of three.

13 Repeat steps 10, 11 and 12 twice more to complete the second of the three-breath colour cycles.

14 Continue with this process of three-breath cycles, invoking each angel of the ray, as follows:

Archangel Michael: blue
Archangel Raphael: green
Archangel Jophiel: yellow
Archangel Gabriel: orange
Archangel Uriel: red

15 When you have finished, either concentrate on breathing in clear white light, or simply relax and let your body come back to everyday reality very slowly.

16 Be aware of any areas of your body that would not absorb some colours, or of any that absorbed lots of colour: these parts of the body may need more attention in the healing process.

**TIP**

*The angels of the rays and their colours are given above in an order that represents a grounding experience, from the fastest colour vibration (violet) to the slowest (red). You could also try the reverse: starting with red and ending with violet, which would be suitable before meditation practice.*

*Part Two*

# THE
# DIRECTORY OF
# HEALING
# ANGELS

# The 21 healing angels

This directory focuses on the 'healing angels' and is divided into three sections: physical, emotional and spiritual healing. The importance of angelic aid in healing yourself and others cannot be over-estimated. When you truly attune yourself by raising your consciousness to the angelic realm, quieten your mind and summon angels to help in every life situation, you may see miracles unfold.

Every angel and Archangel has a special focus, attributes, talents or skills, depending on what that angel is caring for or is in charge of. For instance, the Archangel Chamuel focuses on relationships. He uses the pink ray of spiritual love to heal the inner heart centre. Because the Heart Chakra is closely associated with the expression of love, relationships and compassion, it is naturally considered to be an important centre of nurturing.

Asking for angelic help is entirely logical when you are experiencing challenging life situations. Why should you struggle on alone when God has created the angels to watch over, assist and guide you? The eternal mystery that we call life can seem a long, hard, rough road, which you traverse at your peril. But try to view the gift of life as a positive experience, where even the bad times are good, because you can choose to benefit and learn from each experience by letting yourself grow daily in wisdom, understanding and compassion.

Unfortunately, many people externalize their problems and life experiences on to

others and view the world as a negative place where everyone (and everything) is out to get them. This allows them to grow daily in ignorance, fear, stupidity and intolerance. Some people also avoid spiritual growth by limiting themselves and their expectations. It is easy to identify the way in which their psychological make-up puts up resistance to spiritual growth. The Kabalistic Tree of Life (see page 14–17) can be used as an example of this:

- **Binah** The repression of all spiritual memories.

- **Chesed** The ritualization of spiritual experience, making it routine, ordinary and mundane.

- **Geburah** Religious dogma; one path alone; removing the personal experience of God.

- **Tiphareth** Pessimism; 'I am too old', 'I do not have the time.'

- **Netzach** The overwhelming irrational desire to destroy anything that has beauty.

- **Hod** Over-analysing an experience and intellectualizing it.

- **Yesod** Spiritual experiences being available 'only because of devotion to a guru'.

Once you overcome your psychological resistance to spiritual growth, the journey to enlightenment is worth the effort.

## CONNECTING WITH ARCHANGELS

The following pages will guide you, should you choose to engage with some of the most beloved angels and Archangels, including the four best-known Archangels: Michael, Gabriel, Raphael and Uriel. If you choose this path, the abstract 'idea' of angels will become your reality of God's cosmology and will help you to grasp the otherwise incomprehensible mystery that is God.

God's awesome love is beyond most humans' comprehension, but by studying the different aspects of each Archangel and the ways in which they can help, as they step down the energy of God, you can begin to grasp the sheer beauty and power that humans own as a birthright. Our birthright is a return to 'paradise' or, as it is sometimes known, 'union with God'.

Don't feel daunted at the prospect of this journey. Each journey begins with a single step: the first dawning realization of your divinity, as your higher self (Divine aspect) awakens, by allowing you to connect with your guardian angel (see pages 74–77).

## TEMPLES OF THE ARCHANGELS

In this section of this book you will also learn to visit the spiritual homes of the mighty Archangels. These are known as Temples of Light, Ascension Chambers or Etheric Temples. Some people also know them as Angelic Dream Temples, because they frequently visit them in their 'light body' during sleep.

Each Archangel has a temple 'anchored' in the etheric realm, which lies within the influence of the Earth's planetary grid. These temples are normally situated over the Earth's power vortexes, where many ley lines cross, over remote mountain ranges or small islands, which are often the remains of a larger island or land mass. They may also be situated over sacred sites that are clearly visible on Earth, such as the Egyptian temple at Luxor and the shrine at Fatima in Portugal.

These temples have been used by mystics, initiates and 'spiritual masters' since the dawn of human civilization. They were established by the 'spiritual hierarchy' under the guidance of the Archangels. Each temple has a different focus, function and purpose, which will help you on your evolutionary path. This path is also known as climbing Jacob's ladder, the ladder of light, the Tree of Life, or as ascension into cosmic consciousness or a return to paradise.

The spiritual focus of each temple relates to a 'cosmic virtue' that each Archangel enshrines. When spiritual seekers visit the healing temple during meditation or sleep, they are 'nourished' and inspired by this cosmic virtue.

Each Temple of Light has a different appearance: some are like beautiful Grecian temples, with many gracefully carved stone columns (similar to the Parthenon in Athens, which was erected in 450 BCE to the Greek goddess Pallas Athena); others resemble mighty stone pyramids or other sacred buildings that have existed throughout the Earth's history. However, each Temple of Light is exquisite, with marble or crystal floors and an altar as its centrepiece, where burns the flame of the light ray (colour) on which the Archangel in question focuses.

# HOW TO USE THE DIRECTORY

The following features appear in this section of the book and can be used in different ways as you summon up the healing angels.

- **Invocations** In many of the Archangels' descriptions there is an invocation (a direct appeal for inspiration and guidance), which is designed either to be spoken aloud or said mentally. Invocations may also be used as affirmations (assertions of the truth of something) and repeated mentally to bring about a change in consciousness by removing negative behaviour patterns.

- **Fiats** These are short (but incredibly powerful) affirmations. They are designed to be repeated at least three times, although you could spend five minutes a day saying them. They are meant to be said aloud: your voice is powerful and has the capacity to create or destroy. The Divine intelligence used this power when he said 'Let there be light.' By using your voice, you have the capacity to change your life by connecting more closely with the particular Archangel towards whom the fiat is directed.

- **Decrees** These should be spoken aloud, repeatedly. Each time you say them, you are bringing the 'light' of God into your life. This brings rapid spiritual growth and a swift resolution of any problems. Decrees use the name of God – 'I AM' – which was revealed to Moses when it came out of the burning bush: 'I AM THAT I AM.'

- **Visualizations** You can dramatically increase the power of your invocations, prayers and decrees by maintaining a strong mental picture of what you want to occur. Surrounding the visualization in a sphere of brilliant white light will also increase the power of your visualizations.

- **Meditations** These will help you attune to each Archangel and raise your vibrational rate. Meditation as a daily practice will unleash your immense potential by stimulating harmonious, focused brain activity. This will improve your health by rejuvenating your physical body and activating your 'light body'. It will also clear your mind of stress and improve your powers of concentration, bringing inner peace.

- **Crystals** These are specifically chosen to amplify the colour ray with which the Archangel in question works most closely (for example, emerald for the Archangel Raphael; rose quartz for Chamuel; and ruby for Uriel).

# Guardian angel

**His name means** Personal celestial guide
**Colour** Pastel rainbow colours
**Healing temple** Guides you to all the healing temples
**Crystal** Angel-aura quartz
**Tree of Life** Malkuth
**How he helps** Guides, protects and inspires

Your guardian angel is your personal helper, who has sustained your soul through all your incarnations and who faithfully records all your actions. Your celestial guardian loves you unconditionally and wishes consciously to assist you in raising and refining your vibrational rate.

This angel will help you through all your trials and tribulations, and will comfort, console and encourage you in all your positive endeavours, by helping you to fulfil your life plan and learn all your karmic lessons. You are eternally bonded with your guardian angel as you both evolve together. Your guardian is your primary route to the Godhead and your bridge to all the higher angelic realms.

Your guardian angel is a powerful member of the angelic realm: once you discover your soul connection with your guardian, it will give you faith in yourself and the confidence to move forward with grace and ease. But your angel can never interfere with your free will, even though you may have heard a gentle voice encouraging you in times of personal crisis or despair. Contact with your guardian angel is always positive, bringing feelings of peace, tranquillity and emotional well-being. Some people feel that their guardian is actually their higher self or, as Buddhists call it, the Divine spark or indwelling Buddha-nature.

Everyone also has a guiding angel (see pages 63–65), who inspires you. Guiding angels often change as you evolve spiritually or need to learn different karmic lessons. Some people have several guiding angels working with them at any one time.

## ACTIVATE YOUR ANGELIC CHAKRA

This technique will activate your Angelic Chakra, consciously connecting you with your guardian angel. The Angelic, or Fifth Eye, Chakra is located at the very top of the forehead, and activating it brings angelic attunement, ending the illusion of pain, suffering and duality. Activating (opening) the chakra is central to physical healing, because you become ill in the first place when the chakra is closed and energy flow is restricted.

### YOU WILL NEED
- A small angel-aura quartz crystal (single-terminated)
- A white candle
- Matches or a lighter
- A yoga mat or pad

### WHAT TO DO

1 Cleanse and purify yourself and your energy space (see page 62).

2 Cleanse your crystal before using it (see page 55).

3 Light the white candle and play some soothing music.

4 Lie on the floor, using a yoga mat or pad to make yourself comfortable.

5 Allow your eyes to close.

6 Relax your body (see page 59).

7 Place the crystal on your Angelic Chakra, with the end pointing upwards.

8 Summon your guardian angel, using the following invocation:

*'I now invoke my guardian angel to activate my Angelic Chakra for my conscious connection to the angelic realms of love, light and healing.'*

9 Let angelic light pour into your body through your Crown Chakra – feel it cleansing and nurturing every cell and every fibre of your being with pure consciousness and pure unconditional love. With every inhalation, breathe in the blessings and healing that are meant for you. Feel this pure energy coursing through your body as you receive your angelic blessings.

10 Let the angelic energy bathe your body internally and externally.

11 Feel your guardian angel drawing closer to you, standing before you and activating your Angelic Chakra.

12 Give yourself plenty of time to come back to everyday reality, by becoming aware of your breathing. Feel the weight of your body on the chair or floor. Move your toes and fingers, and let your eyes open slowly. Connect back with the earth (if necessary, imagine roots growing out of the soles of your feet). Close your chakra centres in sequential order, by imagining the petals of a flower closing. Now feel how calm, centred and relaxed you are.

13 Write down your experience in your angel journal (see page 41).

## DISCOVER YOUR
## GUARDIAN ANGEL'S NAME

Traditionally all angels have names, so it is good to know your own guardian angel's name. You can ask for it to be revealed to you: it may come immediately into your mind, or it may be revealed through a dream or meditation practice. However, the easiest way to discover it is to use Scrabble letters or small squares of paper on which you write out every consonant in the alphabet; you could also paint the letters on to small tumbled stones.

### YOU WILL NEED

- A full set of consonants on Scrabble tiles, paper squares or tumbled stones
- A bag for shaking them in
- A white candle
- Matches or a lighter
- A sheet of white writing paper and a pen

### WHAT TO DO

1 Put all the consonants in the bag.

2 Light the white candle and purify your energy space (see page 62).

3 Invoke your guardian angel and ask it to reveal its name to you using the letters.

4 Shake the bag and imagine it filling with angelic light.

5 Now draw out a letter and write it down.

6 Return it to the bag, give it a gentle shake to mix up the letters, then draw out another letter.

7 Once again write down the letter. Continue in this way until you have several letters written down. Your guardian angel will guide you and let you know when you have drawn enough letters for your name.

8 Keeping the consonants in the order in which you drew them from the bag, fill in the spaces between them with vowels, as necessary. Let your guardian angel guide you.

9 When you have come up with a name that feels right, ask your guardian angel for some sign or confirmation that the name is correct.

# Archangel Raphael

**His name means** God has healed
**Colour** Green
**Healing temple** Fatima, Portugal
**Crystal** Emerald
**Tree of Life** Tiphareth
**How he helps** Heals yourself and others

The Archangel Raphael is the healing aspect of the Lord. He is known as the physician of the angelic realm, the Divine healer, for healing yourself and helping you find the inner guidance, love, compassion, balance and inspiration to heal others.

Raphael is one of the seven ruling angels or princes (the word Archangel is not actually found in the Hebrew scriptures), and is one of only three angels to be recognized by the Western Church – the other two being Michael and Gabriel. He is also known as the chief of the guardian angels and as the patron of travellers, and he is often depicted carrying a caduceus (a staff entwined with serpents) or as a pilgrim bearing a staff in one hand and a bowl filled with healing balm in the other.

Raphael's energy is peaceful and healing, although he has the power and authority to cast out demons.

## INVOKE RAPHAEL'S HEALING POWERS

As the overarching angel of healing, the Archangel Raphael has the capacity to guide all healing work, whether this is orthodox or complementary.

- Invoke his assistance to guide the hands of physicians, surgeons and practitioners of complementary medicine.

- Invoke his presence in hospitals, hospices and clinics.

- Invoke his presence to heal rifts between nations, on the battlefield and in areas where there have been natural or manmade disasters.

- Invoke his presence to guide scientists as they search for new cures for diseases.

- Invoke his presence if you are a therapist and need extra guidance.

## USE CRYSTALS FOR SELF-HEALING

The Archangel Raphael brings balance to the Heart Chakra and the ability to experience wholeness and love. His emerald ray encourages you to reach out to others and embrace the world. His energy is restorative and tunes you into the plant kingdom, helping you to understand environmental issues and giving you a social conscience and planetary awareness. Raphael gets to the root of the problem, the very heart of the matter; in fact, he will leave no stone unturned in doing so. This makes him an extremely strong and powerful Archangel – an idealist, who may cause heart palpitations as he delivers you from your demons.

The magical emerald is steeped in mystic lore. In the Bible it is said to be one of the stones used in the breastplate of the high priest. It balances the Heart Chakra and speeds up detoxification, which aids self-healing. It also enhances meditation, removes fear, instils wisdom, increases the intellect and facilitates clarity of understanding. An emerald magnetizes healing energy towards itself, which is why it is so prized by healers.

### YOU WILL NEED

- Three small emeralds (tumble-polished)
- A green candle
- Matches or a lighter
- A yoga mat or pad

### WHAT TO DO

1 Cleanse your crystals before using them (see page 55).

2 Light the green candle and play some relaxing music.

3 Lie on the floor, using a yoga mat or pad to make yourself comfortable.

4 Let your eyes close and your body relax.

5 Mentally call on the Archangel Raphael to oversee the healing process, using the following invocation:

*'Archangel Raphael, guide me as I release all limiting thought patterns that have blighted my soul. I now choose a healthy body, mind and spirit. I am instantly transformed.'*

6 Place one emerald on your Heart Chakra and hold the other two in the palms of your hands. (You can also place an emerald over any area that is filled with pain or needs healing.)

7 Visualize healing energy flowing into your body from your left hand, via your Heart Chakra to your right hand, enabling any pain or tension simply to drain away.

8 Allow 20 minutes for the process to complete itself.

9 Give yourself plenty of time to come back to everyday reality, by earthing and centring yourself (see page 76).

## MEDITATION TO HEAL YOURSELF OR OTHERS

Each Archangel has a spiritual home: a Temple of Light (see page 72) that is anchored over a power spot in the Earth's energy field. The Archangel Raphael's healing temple is anchored over Fatima in Portugal. You can visit his temple often during meditation to receive healing.

You can also ask for someone else who is in need of healing to be taken to Archangel Raphael's temple. It is always wise to ask the person concerned for permission before instigating a healing session for them. If, for some reason, you can't ask their permission, you must place your request under the law of Divine grace and ask that the outcome will be for everyone's highest good.

### WHAT TO DO

1 Sit comfortably, close your eyes and focus on your Heart Chakra.

2 Invoke the Archangel Raphael and ask for his help with healing.

3 Touch your Heart Chakra and direct your awareness inwards, towards the Divine altar of your being.

4 Keep focusing on your Heart Chakra: see it as a glowing emerald flame, and allow this flame to grow steadily larger until it eventually encompasses the whole of your energy field.

5 As the emerald flame purifies your Heart Chakra, you will feel the presence of the Archangel Raphael enfolding you in his wings. Allow him to transport you to his healing temple.

6 When you arrive at the temple, you will be surrounded by the Archangel Raphael's legions of healing angels, who will place you in a healing chamber. If you wish to bring someone else with you for this healing session, see or feel them with you during this meditation process.

7 Healing chambers are often made of white marble. In the centre is a bed (usually formed from pure quartz crystal). Although your logical mind tells you this will be hard and cold, you will always experience it on the angelic planes as warm and comfortable when you lie on it.

8 The healing angels will now use their hands or wings to direct coloured lights, which will bathe your body in the appropriate healing energy.

9 Once the session is complete, let the Archangel Raphael himself or one of his healing angels guide you safely back to your body.

10 Give yourself plenty of time to come back to everyday reality, by earthing and centring yourself (see page 76).

# Archangel Ariel

**His name means** Lion of God
**Colour** Flame-orange
**Healing temple** Tatra Mountains, Poland
**Crystal** Sunstone
**Tree of Life** Malkuth
**How he helps** Aids general health and vitality

Ariel is said to be one of the seven great Archangels and the angel of summer. He is one of Archangel Raphael's most important and steadfast helpers in his quest to free humanity of disease, plagues and pestilence.

The Archangel Ariel is frequently depicted with a lion's head, and people are often surprised by his appearance, especially if he visits them during meditation. He rules over the zodiac sign of Leo, which is represented by a lion. He is sometimes aligned with the Archangel Uriel (see pages 134–137) or confused with the Archangel Auriel (see pages 118–121), although his angelic energy signature could not be further from Auriel's, for she represents the gentle, reflective moon energy while Ariel represents the fire of the sun.

## CRYSTAL TECHNIQUE TO RESTORE EQUILIBRIUM

Ariel brings the energy of the sun to healing situations in his quest to cure vitality-sapping diseases. When you feel tired and exhausted all the time, you lose your enthusiasm for life, your mental and bodily processes become severely compromised, you lose your ability to focus your mind, and your concentration is impaired. You are no longer centred and need to restore your equilibrium.

Sunstone is the Archangel Ariel's natural ally in the crystal kingdom, and it harmonizes the many different levels within the human energy system. It is warming and supportive, bringing in the regenerative power of the sun. It illuminates the Solar Plexus Chakra and reconnects you to your own source of light. Sunstone (just like the Archangel Ariel himself) makes you look at the negative relationships in your life that have caused you to lose your *joie de vivre*. It prevents energy from draining away by removing the ensnarements of others, and transmutes dark, malevolent energy into joyful, life-affirming energy.

## YOU WILL NEED

- Six sunstones (tumble-polished)
- An orange candle
- Matches or a lighter
- A yoga mat or pad
- Some micro-tape (surgical tape, available from pharmacies)

## WHAT TO DO

1 Cleanse your crystals before using them (see page 55).

2 Light the orange candle and play some relaxing music.

3 Lie on the floor, using a yoga mat or pad to make yourself comfortable.

4 Let your eyes close and your body relax.

5 Let your mind follow your breath as you breathe in and out.

6 Mentally call on the Archangel Ariel to oversee this process, using the following invocation:

*'In the name of the Almighty Creator of all, I call upon you, Archangel Ariel, great angel of healing, to restore my health, vitality, creativity and equilibrium.'*

7 Tape a sunstone to the top of each foot, between the tendons of your second and third toes. Place a third sunstone on your Solar Plexus Chakra, another on the Third Eye Chakra, and hold the two remaining sunstones in the palms of your hands.

8 Visualize healing light flowing into your body through your feet, hands and your Solar Plexus and Third Eye Chakras. Allow this energy to bathe your body internally and externally.

9 Allow 20 minutes for the process to complete itself, but be ready to remove the crystals sooner if your intuition tells you that your body has already integrated the energies (sunstone is extremely energizing).

10 Give yourself plenty of time to come back to everyday reality, by earthing and centring yourself (see page 76).

### TIP

*Burning copal (also known as 'lion's tears') is a swift way of summoning the Archangel Ariel. Copal is a gum that is derived from trees that are native to South and Central America. It was burned by the Maya, Aztecs and Incas in their offerings to the gods and is still burned in purification and healing rituals.*

# VISUALIZATION TO RELEASE ENERGY

This visualization uses the powerful transformative properties of the sun to release unwanted energy that has been caused by unresolved emotional issues. These are often situations that you have locked yourself into and that usually require forgiveness or repentance. If these energies are not transformed, they can result in bursts of anger, emotional turmoil or even nervous breakdown.

You can also use this visualization to heal physical conditions, especially ones that have been caused by environmental factors, such as subsonic vibrations, planetary influences, pollution or geopathic stress.

## WHAT TO DO

1 Sit comfortably, close your eyes and focus your awareness inwards.

2 Invoke the Archangel Ariel, asking him to release and transform unwanted energy into positive, life-affirming energy.

3 Touch your Heart Chakra and direct your awareness even deeper inwards, towards the Divine altar of your being.

4 Keep focusing on your Heart Chakra: see it as a glowing orange-gold flame, and let this flame grow steadily larger until it encompasses the whole of your energy field.

5 As the orange flame purifies your heart, you will feel the presence of the Archangel Ariel enfolding you in his wings. Allow him to transport you to the Temple of the Sun.

6 This temple is vast, soaring upwards almost out of sight. The walls are the colour of the sun, infused with a rich, warm amber glow. You are surrounded by seven healing angels, who guide you to the centre of the temple.

7 Upon a dais of seven steps stands the altar of the sun, in the centre of which is a golden rose. The healing angels form a circle around you and the altar. They begin to circle you, moving faster and faster until you can no longer identify any of the angels – all you can see is a great vortex of light that stretches upwards, growing brighter and brighter, becoming ever more intense, until suddenly the angels are gone.

8 Before you now stands the Archangel Ariel, dressed in the yellow-gold robes of the sun. He hands you a beautiful star, which you place on your Solar Plexus Chakra. As you do this, you hear him say, 'Like the mystical phoenix, you are now reborn.'

9 As the healing ceremony is now complete, let the Archangel Ariel guide you back safely to your body.

10 Give yourself plenty of time to come back to everyday reality, by earthing and centring yourself (see page 76).

# Archangel Sabrael

**His name means** His name meaning is secret
**Colour** Green
**Healing temple** Fatima, Portugal
**Crystal** Peridot
**Tree of Life** Tiphareth
**How he helps** Cures disease caused by viruses, parasites or evil spirits

Some sources name Sabrael as one of the seven great Archangels. He is also said to be one of the 'Shining Ones' or 'Choir of Virtues'. He works closely with the Archangel Raphael, who rules over all

matters related to health and healing. The Archangel Sabrael specializes in health problems caused by viruses, parasites or evil spirits. He is also empowered to remove curses and the 'evil eye' when it is thought that demonic energy has been employed by an ill-wisher.

In many ancient traditions, sickness of the body, mind or spirit was thought to be caused by demons or demonic energy that had lodged in the body of the victim. Shamans and other traditional healers used many different methods to extract these evil spirits. Today we understand that disease is caused by viruses, bacteria, genetic make-up, ageing, poor life choices, environmental pollutants and toxins, as well as by poor diet and the stress of modern living. However, if you sincerely believe that your sickness is caused by parasitic energy or evil spirits, call upon the Archangel Sabrael to remove them. The wisdom of the various structures of authority within our current civilization should never be simply accepted without asking questions.

## CRYSTAL TECHNIQUE TO CURE SICKNESS OF BODY, MIND OR SPIRIT

Ideally, you should perform this technique on a Tuesday, when you will be able to harness the powerful energies of Mars to add strength to the Archangel Sabrael. Burn red candles to invoke the strongest possible energy and to enable courage, strength and endurance to empower the Archangel Sabrael.

### PROTECTIVE CRYSTALS

- *Topaz dispels enchantment and makes you invisible in times of emergency.*
- *Amethyst neutralizes negative energy.*
- *Black tourmaline offers grounding and protection.*
- *Peridot drives away evil spirits.*
- *Petalite renders black magic impotent.*
- *Amber breaks spells and enchantments.*
- *Green aventurine is shielding and reflective.*
- *Turquoise protects against the evil eye.*
- *Obsidian banishes demonic entities.*
- *Red coral stops possession by evil spirits and wards off the evil eye.*
- *Aquamarine gives protection against the wiles of the devil.*
- *Actinolite shields against other people's negativity.*
- *Fire agate gives spiritual fortitude.*
- *Ruby promotes courage and spiritual determination.*

### YOU WILL NEED

- Purifying herbs, gums or resins of your choice (see below)
- Sea salt or halite crystals
- Aromatherapy oil of your choice
- Peridot or protective crystals of your choice (see below left)

### WHAT TO DO

1 First, you need to cleanse yourself and your healing space thoroughly (see page 62). Burning powerful purifying herbs, gums and resins is an integral part of this healing ritual. Frankincense, myrrh, copal (see page 84), clove, wormwood, sage and sandalwood are all considered to be protective and purifying and to clear bad energy. They are used in exorcism and for dispelling evil spirits.

2 Take a purifying bath by adding some sea salt or halite crystals (pink or blue) to your bath water. Immerse yourself in the water, with the intention of being purified in heart, body and mind.

3 Get out of the bath, dry yourself and put on clean clothes.

4 Anoint your hands, feet and head with your favourite aromatherapy oil.

5 Try to fast for at least 24 hours, or at least to purify yourself by avoiding red meat, addictive or stimulating substances. Also avoid other sources of stimulation, such as newspapers, magazines, television and the radio. Spend some quiet time in contemplation or meditation, outdoors in nature if possible.

**6** Wear or carry some protective crystals: you could make a protective pouch for some of the crystals that are listed in the box opposite.

**7** It is also important to prepare yourself inwardly by being peaceful, centred, grounded and unafraid.

**8** Call on your guardian angel, and on the Archangels Raphael (who rules over healing the physical body) and Michael (for protection and strength) – after all, you can never have too many angels on your side. Say the following:

'Ask, and it shall be given to you.

Seek, and ye shall find.
Knock, and it shall be opened to you.

For whoever asks, receives;
And he who seeks, finds;
And to him who knocks,
The door is opened.'

**9** You are now ready to summon the Archangel Sabrael, either for yourself or someone else. Using the this petition:

'Behold the light shines in the darkness,
And the darkness cannot overcome it,
In the name of God,
Almighty Creator of all,
I summon you, Archangel Sabrael,
One of the great Shining Ones,
To engage in combat on my behalf,
To cast out the demon of disease from
me ... [name of person]

May your sword of light bring purifying
fire to illuminate every cell in my ...
[name of person's] body,
So that disease has no place to
find refuge,
Fill the chalice of my ... [name of
person's] soul with strength,
Keep my ... [name of person's] body a
temple of God's infinite love
I humbly honour and thank you for
doing your duty,

In the name of God the Almighty.'

**10** Give yourself plenty of time to come back to everyday reality, by earthing and centring yourself (see page 76).

# Archangel Thuriel

**His name means** Angel of the animals
**Colour** Dark greens and browns
**Healing temple** Fatima, Portugal
**Crystals** Green moss agate, Botswana agate
**Tree of Life** Malkuth
**How he helps** Promotes healing in animals; balances humans with nature

Animals, just like humans, suffer a wide range of age-related problems and diseases, being similarly subject to environmental pollutants, toxins, poor diet and the stress of city living. Many pets are also aware of their owner's stress levels and can absorb their owner's emotional problems.

Animals respond favourably to angelic healing and quickly integrate new behavioural patterns. Angelic healing has been used successfully on abused, abandoned or neglected animals, as well as on wild animals and birds. By aligning with the Archangel Thuriel, who harmonizes humans with nature and the elements, you can summon up angelic healing for different planetary species. You can also invoke the following assisting Patron Angels:

- Behemiel: for tame animals

- Hariel: for domestic creatures

- Arael: for birds

- Tubiel: for wild birds

- Nahariel: for creatures of the streams

- Anpiel: for birds

- Manakel: for aquatic creatures

## 'GUIDE' ANIMALS

Some animals are ancient souls, which may come into your life for only a short period of time, often when you need immediate emotional assistance to look at life's bigger picture. They can teach you much about loyalty, humility, gratitude, support and unconditional love. However, because they have a much briefer lifespan than humans, you need to release them with love and gratitude when the time comes for them to move on to the next person who needs their assistance, or when they must progress in their own evolution. I know myself (and have heard similar stories from other people) that some animals become a 'guide' or 'power' animal after their death.

I also believe that helping humans access their inner levels assists animals in their own species' evolution and at the same time enriches humans' experience of the interconnectedness of all life. I had a large ginger cat called Vincent (after Vincent Van Gogh), who had the most enlightened energies I have ever felt and radiated transformational love. His Heart Chakra was a delicate pale pink, which indicated that he was in constant awareness of the fourth and fifth dimensions (levels of higher consciousness, which most animals and humans are unaware of). Sadly, Vincent died in 1992.

Before his death, Vincent became very attuned to crystals and would open the drawer where I kept some of my crystals, 'fish out' his favourite and go to sleep with his head on it. His choice varied, although amethyst was a particular favourite. Soon after his death I met Vincent on the angelic level. He was walking by my side and seemed completely transformed: he was now as large as a lion, with much longer and fluffier ginger fur; but the most amazing change were his large, deep-pink angelic wings.

I am not the only person to have encountered an animal companion who transforms on the angelic level. One lady regularly meets up with her horse, which was dark brown on the earth level, but changed to white on the angelic level.

Another person I know uses her dog as a guide and guardian. The dog regularly appears to me when her owner is in need of healing.

# OFFER HEALING TO YOUR PET

Animals enjoy receiving angelic healing just as much as humans do and normally respond to the healing energies very fast. To treat animals successfully, you need to develop both your observational skills and your empathy. As a general rule, I find that animals tend to communicate in 'pictures'. When I make contact with an animal, I mentally ask it, 'What is wrong?' In return, it shows me in pictorial form what the problem is, although I normally experience its emotions, too. You can develop this sensitivity in time, because everyone has this ability. You might like intuitively to sense your pet's subtle bodies before and after giving a treatment, to establish what changes have taken place.

## WHAT TO DO

1 Use either one or both of your hands and, beginning at your pet's head or feet, allow yourself to be drawn to any area where you are guided.

2 Align yourself with the source of the healing energies you will be using, by invoking the Archangel Thuriel or one of the Patron Angels listed on page 90. You should feel the energy pouring in through your Crown Chakra and down to your Heart Chakra, before flowing down your arms into your hands and flooding out of your palms. Let yourself feel completely surrounded and supported by this energy. You are now ready to transmit the angelic healing towards your pet.

3 Establish contact with your pet by positioning yourself about 30 cm (12 in) away from it.

4 Hold your hands out in front of you, with your palms towards your pet. Let its aura be completely flooded by the healing energy. Spend some time observing how that energy is flowing around it.

5 Let your hands guide you: you might go through the aura layer by layer, or use slow, sweeping movements in the aura. The entire process is intuitive and should take as long as your pet will permit. You will usually know when it has had enough, because it will move away from you or become distracted.

6 You may also feel intuitively guided to work through the chakras, in any order or combination.

7 To work on your pet's physical body, let yourself be guided to either its head or feet. You can work directly over an injury or wound, if necessary. The length of time that you keep your hands in each position is up to you, although animals generally absorb healing energy very quickly.

**TIP**

*Sometimes you will be more successful if you give a distant healing session (see page 97); you can also augment a 'hands-on' session with distant healing.*

# Archangel Sandalphon

**His name means** Derived from the Greek, possibly meaning 'co-brother'
**Colour** Rainbow colours
**Healing temple** Mountains of Andalucia, southern Spain
**Crystal** Fulgurite
**Tree of Life** Malkuth
**How he helps** Promotes distance healing and planetary group healing

The Archangel Sandalphon is guardian of the Earth and is personally responsible for the welfare of humankind. He is in charge of Earth healing, distance healing and planetary group work. He is also in command of choosing the gender of a child when it is conceived and of protecting all unborn babies.

Sandalphon unites Heaven and Earth, his role being to carry the prayers of humans up to God. With Archangel Metatron (see pages 154–157), he represents the twin reflection of the Divine. As twins, they are the Alpha and Omega, the beginning and the end: their presence recalls the esoteric expression 'As above, so below'.

There is an ancient tradition that Sandalphon once took human form as the prophet Elijah (just as Metatron was once the prophet Enoch). His presence is always in the Kingdom (the Earthly plane), and he does not move between the planes of existence, for he is so tall that his energy spans all levels of the Tree of Life. The Talmud (the primary source of Jewish religious law) states that 'Sandalphon's head reaches heaven', while Moses described him as the 'tall angel'.

## HEALING MEDITATION

The Archangel Sandalphon resonates with all the colours of the rainbow. Summon him and visit his healing temple to develop balance, harmony and stability in your life.

### WHAT TO DO

1 Sit comfortably, close your eyes and focus on your Heart Chakra.

2 Call upon the Archangel Sandalphon, using the following invocation:

*'Archangel Sandalphon, guardian of planet Earth and holder of the sacred presence, please support my pranic life-force. Help me reclaim my rainbow soul mandala and my original genetic blueprint by activating my latent DNA strands. Begin the process of activating, birthing and anchoring my Light-Body on to planet Earth.'*

3 Touch your Heart Chakra and direct your awareness inwards. As you focus on your Heart Chakra, see it as a glowing rainbow flame: let this flame grow larger until it encompasses the whole of your body and your aura.

4 Let yourself feel completely surrounded, supported and nurtured by this energy. You will often see it as a sphere of rainbow-coloured light. As the flame purifies your energy field, you will feel the presence of the Archangel Sandalphon enfolding you in his wings. Let him transport you to his healing temple in southern Spain.

5 When you arrive at the temple, you will be surrounded by Sandalphon's angels, who will place you in a healing chamber.

6 The healing angels will use their hands or wings to direct coloured lights, which will bathe your body in the appropriate healing energy.

7 Once the session is complete, let the Archangel Sandalphon or one of his healing angels guide you safely back to your body.

8 Give yourself plenty of time to come back to everyday reality, by earthing and centring yourself (see page 76).

# PLANETARY AND DISTANT HEALING MEDITATION

When you are channelling planetary healing, try not to suppress your emotions, because this can cause blockages in your subtle bodies and affect your health. Instead, focus fully on the emotions created within you by the haunting images you have seen. This will direct healing energy to the places where it is most needed and should ease any feelings of distress that you are experiencing.

## WHAT TO DO

1 Sit comfortably on the floor or in a chair.

2 Visualize roots growing out of the soles of your feet to ground and strengthen you.

3 Breathe easily and naturally, to ensure that your own energy circuits are open and flowing smoothly.

4 Summon the Archangel Sandalphon, aligning yourself with his energy. You should feel the energy flowing in through your Crown Chakra, down into your Heart Chakra, then flowing down your arms and out of your palms.

5 Let yourself feel completely surrounded, supported and nurtured by this energy, which you will often see as a sphere of rainbow-coloured light.

6 If it seems appropriate, also let the healing energy flow downwards from your Heart Chakra into your Solar Plexus, Sacral and Root Chakras. You are now ready to transmit this energy.

7 Visualize it as a swirling rainbow of light moving out from your body towards the area of affliction to which you have chosen to direct it. See the people who are affected absorbing this healing energy (you will notice the area becoming illuminated with a rainbow light).

8 As you continue to watch, you will become aware of other healers and planetary healing groups who are also sending out rainbows of hope. These people are the children of light: the 'rainbow warriors'.

9 Let your energy fuse with theirs. Feel the healing power intensifying as everyone joins together. Many of these children of light meditate every day to send out healing energy in the form of rainbows; they instinctively know that those in need will receive it in a form that is appropriate to them. You should now feel a part of this angelically guided energy.

10 You can choose to send distant healing to a family member, friend or loved one, knowing that the energy they receive is blessed many times over, due to the unconditional healing being sent by other healers and healing groups.

11 When you feel ready, detach yourself from the energy of the Archangel Sandalphon.

12 Give yourself plenty of time to come back to everyday reality, by earthing and centring yourself (see page 76), giving thanks for the experience.

# Archangel Chamuel

**His name means** He who sees God
**Colour** Pink
**Healing temple** St Louis, Missouri, USA
**Crystal** Rose quartz
**Tree of Life** Geburah
**How he helps** Heals relationships

The Archangel Chamuel (Khamael) helps you renew and improve loving, caring relationships with others by developing your Heart Chakra. This is accomplished through the beautiful pink ray that represents your ability to love and nurture others and to give and receive love unconditionally and free of self-interest. It is a love that transcends and transforms the self and that moves you through compassion towards a Divine state of emotional maturity. Many people are afraid of opening their Heart Chakra, but those who have been able to overcome this fear have a charismatic warmth, which others find reassuring, soothing and uplifting.

Chamuel assists you in all your relationships, especially during life-changing situations. He helps you to appreciate the loving relationships that you already have in your life. His message is: 'It is only the love energy within any given purpose that gives lasting value and benefit to all creation.' Reach out to this Archangel also for immediate practical assistance and protection against the energies of anti-love, such as cruelty, slander, malice or jealousy.

## CRYSTAL TECHNIQUE TO STRENGTHEN A RELATIONSHIP

This technique will enable you to renew or start a loving, caring relationship.

### YOU WILL NEED
- Two rose quartz crystals (tumble-polished)

### WHAT TO DO
1 Cleanse your crystals before using them (see page 55), then charge them with loving, harmonious energy.

2 Keep one for yourself and give the other crystal to the person with whom you wish to build a strong relationship. If it is impractical to give them the crystal (due to divorce, separation or bereavement), keep both crystals on your angelic altar (see pages 42–43) and ask the angels of love to harmonize the relationship for everyone's highest good.

## USE CRYSTALS TO BUILD SELF-LOVE

The Archangel Chamuel is directly concerned with building confidence and self-esteem. He will quickly dissolve the negative emotions of self-condemnation, low self-worth, self-loathing and selfishness. He will also ignite your inner happiness by showing you your own unique talents and abilities and, perhaps more important, will show you how to nurture these attributes and value yourself.

### YOU WILL NEED
- Three small rose quartz crystals (tumble-polished)
- Some micro-tape (surgical tape, available from pharmacies)

### WHAT TO DO

1 Cleanse your crystals before using them (see page 55).

2 Invoke the Archangel Chamuel to oversee the process. Then allow yourself to think about your beliefs concerning yourself, your self-doubts, self-sabotage, self-image and so on.

3 Place one crystal on your Heart Chakra and the other two on the sides of your forehead, using micro-tape to hold them in position.

4 The process is complete when you feel a change of emotion or when you experience feelings of harmony, peace or inner happiness. Use this technique often to build up your self-esteem.

## MEDITATION TO ATTRACT A SOULMATE

Seeking a soulmate is a universal quest and the most precious experience of human love. The Archangel Chamuel can assist you in finding your true soulmate – someone with whom you can share your innermost thoughts, feelings and emotions. To receive angelic blessings on your quest you must feel comfortable within yourself and relinquish all ideas of controlling and manipulating the energy of love by stepping into the harmonious energy of partnership and equality.

### WHAT TO DO

1 Sit comfortably, close your eyes and focus on your Heart Chakra.

2 Invoke the Archangel Chamuel, asking for your heart to be cleansed of negative emotional beliefs concerning the energy of love. This allows your heart to be receptive when your soulmate arrives.

3 Keep focusing on your Heart Chakra: visualize it as a glowing pink flame. As your heart energy purifies you sufficiently to attract a soulmate, you will see a beam of golden light shooting outwards from your Heart Chakra.

4 You will become aware of all the souls on the planet, but your heart beam will go directly to your soulmate. Visualize him or her awakening, becoming aware of you and beginning to move swiftly in your direction. This allows your paths to cross. You have now started the process of meeting your soulmate.

## INVOCATION TO HEAL A BROKEN HEART

Falling in love is an all-consuming experience, but when the object of your affection falls out of love with you it can be devastating. You may be filled with grief and feelings of abandonment. These negative emotions wound your heart and create barriers that stop loving energy from flowing into your life. Although you may yearn to release painful past experiences so that you can form new relationships, you are probably fearful of letting go, of losing control and of being hurt again.

Dreams are an excellent way of working with angels. Each Archangel has a spiritual home, an ascension Temple of Light that is anchored over a power spot in the Earth's energy field. Archangel Chamuel's healing temple is anchored over St Louis, Missouri. You can visit this temple often during your dreams so that you can heal your broken heart and allow your Heart Chakra to be transformed by love.

### WHAT TO DO

1 Write down on a piece of paper that you have chosen to visit the dream temple of the Archangel Chamuel. List what you wish to achieve during the experience and place the paper under your pillow.

2 Get into bed and relax. Let your mind follow your breathing as you gently breathe in and out.

3 Turn your focus to your Heart Chakra, where your spirit resides, and mentally call on the Archangel Chamuel, using the following invocation:

*'Archangel Chamuel, ignite and expand
the flame of love within my heart.
Dissolve any resistance and fear I
may have to allowing unconditional
love for myself and others to heal my
broken heart.'*

4 When you fall asleep you will travel to Archangel Chamuel's temple and receive his help, comfort and guidance. In the morning, you will wake up feeling joyful and positive. Perhaps you will even remember your dream.

# Archangel Muriel

**Her name means** Angel of the sea
**Colour** Aquamarine
**Healing temple** The sea
**Crystals** Aquamarine, pearl
**How she helps** Heals emotional turmoil

Archangel Muriel is guardian angel of the zodiac sign of Cancer, which rules the month of June, and the sign of Cancer is allied to the energies of the moon. The moon in turn controls the tides of the sea and, like a mirror, reflects your emotions back to you. Just like your emotions, the sea can be calm and tranquil or tumultuous and stormy.

The Archangel Muriel's energy is sensitive, loving, supportive and nurturing. She teaches you to be aware of the needs of others, but also to honour your own emotional needs. She helps you get in touch with your feelings, and guides you in developing your awareness of subtle energies. She brings gentle, harmonious healing to those who are emotionally insecure or who are dreamy or subject to mood swings.

The many species of animals, fish and plants, the minerals and the birds that fly between Heaven and Earth are a unique expression of the vision of God. They were brought into being by the numerous angels whose sense of beauty interpreted the dream of the Eternal Artist by creating this wondrously beautiful planet. All natural phenomena have tremendous potential to heal through their sacred powers. In the shamanic tradition, when you journey to the inner levels you seek out your 'Power Animal' or guide. This ally is wholly reliable on all levels and acts very much like your guiding angel. Muriel has a special affinity with dolphins and whales.

## MEDITATION TO RELEASE EMOTIONAL BLOCKAGES

The oceans and its inhabitants have amazing healing and rebirthing powers – as those who have swum with dolphins will attest to. In the animal kingdom, each animal possesses a physical body, an etheric body and a soul, as well as its own personality – as anyone who owns a pet will testify. Animals differ from humans in that each species has a collective higher self: a group mind that is shared by each member. This group mind is overshadowed by that species' spirit or guardian angel. You can use this spirit to help you release emotional turmoil.

### WHAT TO DO

1 Sit comfortably, close your eyes and focus on your Heart Chakra.

2 Invoke the Archangel Muriel and ask for healing and higher-self alignment.

3 Touch your Heart Chakra and direct your awareness inwards, towards the Divine altar of your being.

4 Keep focusing on your Heart Chakra: see it as a glowing aquamarine flame, then allow this flame to grow steadily larger until it encompasses the whole of your body and aura.

5 As the aquamarine flame gently purifies your Heart Chakra, you become aware of the presence of the Archangel Muriel as she enfolds you in her wings and transports you to her healing temple.

6 Muriel's etheric temple stands on a beautiful white sandy beach. The sun is shining; the deep aquamarine sea is perfectly clear; the sky is blue, with delicate white, feathery angel clouds.

7 In the distance you see a group of dolphins swimming. These are joyful creatures, who teach you about harmony and connecting to your higher self.

8 You decide to wade out into the water towards them. One of the dolphins sees you and gleefully approaches. As it does so, you feel more peaceful and begin to relax deeply.

9 Let yourself swim with your dolphin: feel its joy and harmony, and allow yourself to absorbs these emotions. Dolphins are telepathic – your dolphin is aware of your needs, so feel yourself being nurtured by its energy as it gently instructs you to release stored emotional turmoil and blockages. You quickly begin to feel lighter in spirit, reborn and refreshed.

10 Stay swimming with the dolphins as long as you like, or until you feel have absorbed all the delicate aquamarine ray of healing that you need. When you are ready, let the Archangel Muriel guide you safely back to your body.

11 Give yourself plenty of time to come back to everyday reality, by earthing and centring yourself (see page 76).

12 Write down your experience in your angel journal (see page 41).

# CRYSTAL HEALING TECHNIQUE

Aquamarine, the 'gem of the sea', derives its name from sea water. Legend says that it is the treasure of mermaids, with the power to keep sailors safe at sea. Aquamarine is calming and soothing on all levels, swiftly releasing blockages as it washes away anger, guilt, hatred, resentment, fear or sorrow. It has a strong affinity with those who are highly attuned to subtle energies and acts as a stone of courage by filtering out discordant energy. It aligns all the chakras and facilitates communication with the angelic realm. It also enhances psychic skills, in particular the ability to tune into images from the past or other dimensions.

## YOU WILL NEED

- Six aquamarine crystals (tumble-polished)
- An aquamarine or pale turquoise candle
- Matches or a lighter
- A yoga mat or pad

## WHAT TO DO

1 Cleanse your crystals before using them (see page 55).

2 Light the aquamarine or turquoise candle and play some relaxing music.

3 Lie on the floor, using a yoga mat or pad to make yourself comfortable.

4 Let your eyes close and your body relax.

5 Mentally call on the Archangel Muriel to oversee the healing process, using the following invocation:

**TIP**

*Sleeping with an aquamarine crystal under your pillow enhances dream recall, counteracts negative forces and facilitates angelic contact.*

*'Archangel Muriel, guide me as I release painful personal memories and hidden blockages that have stopped me achieving my goals.'*

6 Place the six crystals evenly around your body: one beneath your feet, one above your head, and two on either side of the body, level with your elbows and knees.

7 Visualize the healing energy entering and filling your body.

8 Allow 20 minutes for the process to complete itself, but be ready to remove the crystals sooner if your intuition tells you to.

9 Give yourself plenty of time to come back to everyday reality, by earthing and centring yourself (see page 76).

# Archangel Jophiel

**His name means** Beauty of God
**Colour** Golden-yellow
**Healing temple** Lanchow, China
**Crystal** Citrine
**Tree of Life** Hod
**How he helps** Promotes wisdom

Jophiel (Jofiel or Zophiel) is the Archangel of wisdom, who works with the angels from the Halls of Wisdom. His yellow-gold solar ray is often called the 'sunshine ray'.

## ENERGY RENEWAL

Call on the Archangel Jophiel:

- If your energy is low and you have lost your *joie de vivre*.

- If you feel unclear or confused, or your thoughts are scattered.

- If you feel you have lost your inner light.

- If you suffer from SAD (seasonal affective disorder).

- If you feel burdened by worries.

- If you feel you have lost your personal power and sense of self.

- If you need to boost your confidence, enthusiasm and self-esteem.

- If you need to recover 'soul fragments' due to illness or shock.

- If you need to release negative thought patterns or addictive behaviour traits.

- If you are fearful and full of self-doubt.

## INSPIRATION

Summon the Archangel Jophiel:

- If you feel creatively blocked or your creativity needs a boost.

- If you need a fresh approach to life.

- If you get lost in thoughts and fantasies.

- If you wish to get flashes of insight for problem-solving.

- If you feel torn by inner conflicts, to remove tension and stress from the body.

- If you require mental clarity, or when you have to take an examination.

## WISDOM

Invoke the Archangel Jophiel:

- If you seek connection to your higher self.

- If you seek inner peace and guidance.

- If you need to integrate new spiritual abilities.

- If you seek inner wisdom.

- If you wish to develop your intuition.

- If you need to connect to the etheric realms.

## UNDERSTANDING

Call on the Archangel Jophiel:

- If you have difficulty understanding yourself.

- If you have trouble comprehending others.

- If you have difficulty integrating different aspects of your personality.

- If you need to throw some light on a difficult situation.

- If you need to absorb new information and skills.

- If you suffer from paranoia or are self-absorbed.

- If you wish to understand yourself at a deeper level.

## FIATS TO THE ARCHANGEL JOPHIEL

- Archangel Jophiel, fill my life with light, joy and laughter.

- Archangel Jophiel, awaken my soul from its slumber.

- Archangel Jophiel, inspire me with your wisdom.

- Archangel Jophiel, strengthen my connection to my higher self.

- Archangel Jophiel, charge my whole being with light.

## DECREE TO THE ARCHANGEL JOPHIEL

I AM, I AM, I AM the wisdom flame of illumination.

## HEALING TECHNIQUE TO ENHANCE ENERGY

This technique will bring renewed energy and joy into your life.

### WHAT TO DO

1 Cleanse your hands by washing them in warm water, then dry them thoroughly. This process purifies the emotions.

2 Call on the Archangel Jophiel and ask him to assist you.

3 Begin to sensitize your hands by shaking them vigorously. This releases any blocked energy. Briskly rub them together to concentrate the energy into them.

4 Hold your hands with your palms facing each other, about 25 cm (10 in) apart. Feel the energy radiating and vibrating between them – play with this energy.

5 Begin to form this energy into a sphere and visualize it being sunshine-yellow in colour. Ask the Archangel Jophiel to empower the energy with his light.

6 When it feels right, place this yellow ball in your solar plexus area. This energizes your mental body, bringing energy renewal, spiritual elevation, illumination and joy.

7 Give yourself plenty of time to come back to everyday reality, by earthing and centring yourself (see page 76).

## CRYSTAL TECHNIQUE TO DRAW IN SUNSHINE

Citrine removes fear, anxiety, worry, confusion and indecision. It clears the mind and eases nervous exhaustion, stress, burn-out, panic attacks, hot flushes and digestive disorders, and improves the functioning of the immune system. Citrine instils a positive attitude – it harmonizes, brightens and brings illumination.

### YOU WILL NEED

- A natural citrine crystal (single-terminated)
- A yoga mat or pad

### WHAT TO DO

1 Cleanse your crystal before using it (see page 55).

2 Lie on the floor, using a yoga mat or pad to make yourself comfortable.

3 Invoke the Archangel Jophiel to oversee the process.

4 Place the point of the citrine on your Solar Plexus Chakra, with the termination pointing upwards.

5 Visualize the healing energy entering and filling your body.

6 Begin with a short session of five minutes. If your energy is very depleted or you are studying, you can extend the time accordingly.

7 Give yourself plenty of time to come back to everyday reality, by earthing and centring yourself (see page 76).

## VISUALIZATION FOR ILLUMINATION

This visualization will help bring you inspiration when you feel emotionally blocked.

### WHAT TO DO

1 Sit comfortably, close your eyes and focus your awareness inwards.

2 Call upon the Archangel Jophiel to oversee the process.

3 Visualize a golden-yellow light flowing into the top of your head.

4 See it flooding the whole of your body and aura with light.

5 Allow the light to form a sphere of light around you.

6 Breathe in the golden-yellow light and see it filling you with energy, life-force and inspiration.

7 Visualize the darkness, negativity and stress dissolving in the light.

8 Give yourself plenty of time to come back to everyday reality, by earthing and centring yourself (see page 76).

# Archangel Haniel

**His name means** Glory of God or Grace of God
**Colour** Turquoise
**Healing temple** Tibet
**Crystal** Turquoise
**Tree of Life** Netzach
**How he helps** Assists in overcoming emotional turmoil, and helps you when you need encouragement or justice

Haniel is the Archangel of Divine communication through clear perception. He is a *warrior* angel; his authority assists you to fulfil your 'soul's mission', which is to praise, honour, love and reunite with God by using and trusting in your own great God-connectedness, which will in turn inspire others.

Invoke the Archangel Haniel to give you strength and perseverance when you feel weak. He will guide you through visions, personal revelations and angelic coincidences. Haniel is also the protector of your soul and promotes the virtue of determination.

## OVERCOME OBSTACLES

The Archangel Haniel is a Dharmapala, a protector of the Dharma: your own truth and God-reality, which, when followed with steadfast faith, is conducive to gaining enlightenment. Call on him when you feel that life is difficult and you are beset by obstacles (even the dark forces of negativity), and he will provide the spiritual armour necessary for your salvation.

His colour is turquoise-blue, which invokes the essence of *shunyata* – the infinite blue emptiness that radiates in all directions, absolutely clear, pristine and glorious. Through this turquoise sky stretching to infinity you can gain an understanding of the expansiveness and true soul-freedom that could be yours: if you do not allow your horizons to become narrow, dull, clouded and limited; if you do not permit your mind to become fixated by cravings and worries, centred on what are really passing phenomena. In reality, your little lifespan is but a nano-second in the scheme of eternity, and you should not dull your mind with trivial concerns but instead devote yourself to spiritual pursuits.

## SEEK JUSTICE AND ANGELIC ALIGNMENT

Summon the Archangel Haniel when you require justice, for his energy is uplifting and he aligns you with your own greatness. He brings down a pillar of light, which will sustain you through the 'dark night of the soul' when you doubt yourself and your own values or feel unworthy of God's infinite love. If you work constantly with Haniel, he will transform you into a pillar of light, into a beacon towards which others will be drawn.

As you – and every other human – connect and align to your own God-self, you raise the vibration of the Earth, allowing her peaceful transition into the Age of Aquarius. This vibrational shift started with the 'Harmonic Convergence' that occurred in 1987 and is due to be fulfilled by the year 2012. This is an amazing time to be incarnate on the planet Earth as she makes her transition into the higher dimensions of light.

Those who hold the light, and live in the light, will become part of the 'Family of Light'. You must have the clear intention and the childlike humility to become more than you have ever thought possible – this applies even to those people who have studied for years in this lifetime and could be considered adepts. If you ever consider yourself an adept, you have failed, because you have taken on a fixed horizon: a fixed persona that will limit your potential to become a multi-dimensional being of pure unconditional love – and by becoming the living embodiment of unconditional love, you will unite all the aspects of God. This is your purpose for living; you must never become blinded by your own light, your own self-importance. By the same token you must never make yourself smaller than you truly are, or limit your potential to change the world.

## RELEASE EMOTIONAL RESTRICTIONS

Summon the Archangel Haniel to view the areas of your life where you have chosen to restrict yourself or have given away your freedom. You should look at the multitude of restrictions that you have taken upon yourself and that have stifled your voice, your channel or communication, your opinions and your choices. You must never become compliant and select the easy option, because this will restrict your spiritual growth and limit your fields of perception. As you begin to experience the massive infusion of Archangel Haniel's light and feel the changes that are upon you, you must remind yourself of the exquisite possibilities that are placed before you and let yourself choose wisely and for the highest good of all.

## CRYSTAL TECHNIQUE FOR SOUL EXPRESSION

This technique facilitates emotional freedom, confidence and inner strength. It will calm the nerves and act as natural tranquillizer. This in turn will ease emotional turmoil and enable the blossoming of your soul expression through heartfelt communication.

### YOU WILL NEED

- Seven turquoise crystals (tumble-polished)
- A yoga mat or pad

### WHAT TO DO

1 Cleanse your crystals before using them (see page 55).

2 Lie on the floor, using a yoga mat or pad to make yourself comfortable.

3 Call upon the Archangel Haniel to oversee the process, using the following invocation:

*'Archangel Haniel, warrior and protector of the Dharma, keep my feet for ever on the path towards full enlightenment of my soul. Encourage me when I feel weak, disillusioned or beset by obstacles. Reveal to me the grace of God, and renew my spiritual armour so that my soul will find true salvation and enlightenment.'*

4 Place six of the turquoises evenly around your body: one directly above your head, one beneath and between your feet, and one level with each knee and elbow.

Place the seventh on your witness point (thymus), midway between the Heart and Throat Chakras.

5 Visualize the healing energy entering and filling your body.

6 Begin with a short session of five minutes.

7 Give yourself plenty of time to come back to everyday reality, by earthing and centring yourself (see page 76).

# Archangel Michael

**His name means** Who is as God or Who can stand against God
**Colour** Sapphire-blue
**Healing temple** Banff, near Lake Louise, Canada
**Crystals** Lapis lazuli, blue sapphire, kyanite
**Tree of Life** Hod
**How he helps** Offers immediate protection, releases fears and phobias, strengthens your faith

The mighty Archangel Michael is the protector of humanity, the supreme and incorruptible commander-in-chief of all the Archangels. He leads the heavenly forces, his 'legions of light', against evil (the demonic-inspired human vices of anger, hatred, negativity, cruelty, hostility and conflict).

Michael can appear simultaneously in three of the Seven Heavens, and Islamic, Jewish and Christian holy scriptures all venerate him. His main colour is sun-yellow (in fact, the fiery power of the solar plexus is his domain), but because he carries a sword made of a sapphire-blue flame, he is often associated with the empowerment and development of the Throat and Third Eye Chakras. This ray represents both the power and the will of God, as well as the powers of faith, protection and truth.

The Archangel Michael is a being of magnificent, awe-inspiring glory and radiant light, who is frequently depicted riding a white horse (representing pure, pristine, spiritual power) while in the act of thrusting a lance into a writhing serpent (which is usually on the ground beneath his feet). This shows Michael symbolically slaying the lower aspect of the human personality, where fear and restriction reside, enabling the higher-mind connection of the soul to emerge phoenix-like, as the winged dragon of ultimate wisdom.

## USE CRYSTALS TO RELEASE FEARS AND PHOBIAS

This healing technique is accomplished with the loving help and angelic protection of the Archangel Michael and his Legions of Light. It releases fears, phobias and unease. It also gives you freedom from the nagging fear of self-doubt, and strengthens your faith in God and in yourself by instilling inner fortitude. Physically it strengthens the immune and meridian systems by activating the Hara centre.

The Hara is not a traditional chakra in the Hindu system; in fact, the word comes from the Japanese language (you may have heard it before, in the term for Japanese ritual suicide, *hara-kiri*. It relates to a very powerful energy centre, which is located three finger-widths below the navel. When the Hara is damaged or breached, the life-force is released very quickly. This energy centre is vitally important in both men and women. It is concerned with issues of mental and emotional stability, good health, stamina, personal life-force and healthy boundaries. It also plays a direct role in creativity, joy and abundance.

Begin with a short session of about five minutes.

### YOU WILL NEED

- 12 clear quartz crystals (natural single-terminated)
- Three lapis lazuli, blue sapphire or kyanite crystals (natural or tumble-polished)
- A yoga mat or pad

### WHAT TO DO

1 Cleanse your crystals before using them (see page 55).

2 Lie on the floor, using a yoga mat or pad to make yourself comfortable.

3 Invoke the Archangel Michael to oversee the process:

*'Mighty Archangel Michael, empower me. I acknowledge that I have free will, so I now choose a life-path of freedom and joy. I ask that this is done lovingly with the help and protection of your 'legions of light'. I call on you now in my hour of need for total protection, strength, fearlessness and cutting the cords that bind my soul in ignorance. Give me freedom from the fear of self-doubt, reinforce my faith, bring inner strength and outer courage.'*

4 Place the quartz crystals evenly around your body, one directly above your head and one directly beneath and between your feet, with the terminations pointing outwards.

5 Position the three lapis lazuli crystals as follows: at the Throat and Third Eye Chakras and at the Hara point.

6 Visualize the healing energy entering and filling your body.

7 Give yourself plenty of time to come back to everyday reality, by earthing and centring yourself (see page 76).

## CRYSTAL TECHNIQUE TO SUMMON PROTECTION

This exercise brings immediate practical assistance, giving you a mantle of protection from physical and spiritual dangers.

### YOU WILL NEED

- Seven lapis lazuli, blue sapphire or kyanite crystals (natural or tumble-polished)
- A yoga mat or pad

### WHAT TO DO

1 Cleanse your crystals before using them (see page 55).

2 Lie on the floor, using a yoga mat or pad to make yourself comfortable.

3 Invoke the Archangel Michael to place his cloak of protection around you.

4 Place six of the crystals evenly around your body: one directly above your head, one beneath and between your feet, and one level with each knee and elbow. Put the seventh on your Third Eye Chakra.

5 Visualize the healing energy entering and filling your body.

### TIP

*You can also imagine the Archangel Michael's cloak of protection around you. Visualize a deep blue cloak with a hood that covers you (or a loved one) completely from head to foot.*

6 Stay in the crystal energy until you feel a change of emotion and until the uneasy sensations have left you.

7 Give yourself plenty of time to come back to everyday reality, by earthing and centring yourself (see page 76).

## FIATS TO THE ARCHANGEL MICHAEL

You can summon the Archangel Michael at any time to give you immediate protection.

- Archangel Michael, help me! Help me! Help me!
- Archangel Michael, protect me from all harm.
- Archangel Michael, protect me from psychic attack.

## VISUALIZE THE SWORD OF PROTECTION

You can also visualize the sapphire-blue flame sword of the Archangel Michael cutting away darkness, fear, negativity, phobias and binding ties. Each time you do this you empower yourself with the energy, integrity and authority of the Archangel Michael. To close the visualization, ask him to wrap you in his deep blue cloak of protection.

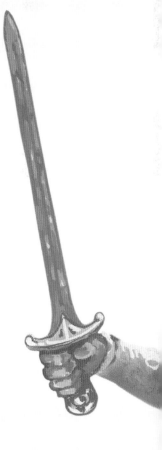

# Archangel Auriel

**Her name means** Light of God
**Colour** Silver
**Healing temple** Moon
**Crystal** Moonstone
**Tree of Life** Malkuth
**How she helps** Harmonizes the female aspect of your personality, accessing the deep subconscious and releasing fears

The Archangel Auriel is the feminine aspect of Uriel (Oriel) (see pages 134–137). She can also be thought of as the Archangel Uriel's female companion – the bride. She is often called the Angel of Destiny because, just like Uriel, if invoked she will illuminate your path through life and show you your destiny. The Archangel Auriel works exclusively through the mysterious reflective energy of the moon, so she is also known as the 'lunar angel'.

## MOON MAGIC

The changing faces of the moon as she waxes and wanes, as she silently compels the ebbing and flowing of the seas and oceans, as she regulates the tides of birth, growth and decay, as she awakens the secret dreams of humanity, have always been seen as magical.

Physically, the moon exerts a gravitational pull on the waters of the Earth. Humans are made up of more than 90 per cent water, so when high tide is reached at full moon we are affected by strange things stirring in the depths of our psyche. Then the deep subconscious has a tendency to surface, often through dreams, visions, hallucinations or nightmares. Each month our psychic power increases at the time of the full moon, when the 'veil' between worlds is at its thinnest and when our natural gifts of clairvoyance (second sight), clairsentience (supernatural feeling) and clairaudience (supernatural hearing) are enhanced.

The moon has two great tides of waxing and waning: waxing from the new moon to the full moon, and waning from the full moon to the dark moon. On the 'night of no moon' the moon seems to disappear. The complex lunar cycle consists of 28 days, and in ancient texts is referred to as the 28 Mansions of the Moon.

## SUN AND MOON DISCS IN HARMONY

At each full moon, the sun and moon are in balance, and the moon becomes the 'magic mirror' of the sun's disc. We can harmonize our personalities by balancing our male and female polarities. However, because humans live in a left-brain, analytical, scientific society where the feminine right brain (intuition) is suppressed, this balance is viewed with suspicion, fear and even dread, because of the changes it will bring.

The physical moon receives her light and energy from the sun and reflects it to the Earth. This light is meant to illuminate and awaken our souls, so at full moon we are receiving maximum soul light – hence the increase in psychic abilities. In mystic law the moon is known as the 'world soul'.

The masculine left brain is logical and analytical. It is meant to support the feminine right-brain, intuitive side (the soul) by keeping the physical body alive using survival skills  so that humans can be a living bridge between Heaven and Earth. This represents the alchemical marriage of sun and moon, or the marriage of the physical male (the groom) with the spiritual female (the bride). When your feminine, intuitive side is not supported (nurtured), it becomes wounded (resulting in emotional turmoil), and this is reflected in your personality as fears and phobias. Fears and phobias stunt your spiritual growth, stifle your dreams.

## USE CRYSTALS TO CALL DOWN THE MOON

This technique will connect you with your deep subconscious mind. It is designed to release fears and phobias, enhancing and harmonizing the feminine, intuitive aspect of your personality. You should undertake it on a Monday, because this is the day of the week dedicated to the moon. It is also more powerful when done at a full moon and repeated each full moon, as some energies (negative experiences, fears and phobias) are harder to shift than others.

This exercise uses moonstones, the premier female power-stones and the talisman of the goddess. Moonstones increase and support your intuitive abilities, quickly stabilizing all emotional states and releasing stress and tension, especially from the Sacral Chakra. Because negative emotions are being released from your physical body and aura, you may experience an unpleasant taste in your mouth, but this is a good sign that you are expelling negative experiences.

### YOU WILL NEED

- 13 moonstones (tumble-polished) to represent the lunar cycles of the year
- A purifying bath with sea salt or halite crystal
- White clothes to wear (in sacred angelic lore, black is never worn)
- Frankincense or a specially prepared moon incense
- White flowers, such as lilies
- A silver or white candle (in a silver or glass holder)
- Matches or a lighter
- A white sheet

## WHAT TO DO

1 Cleanse your crystals before using them (see page 55).

2 Take a purifying bath, then put on some white clothes, light some frankincense or moon incense, and arrange your white flowers to attract the moon angels.

3 Light the candle and listen to some soothing music.

4 Lie down comfortably on the floor on the white sheet, to aid the cleansing process.

5 Summon the Archangel Auriel and ask her to surround you with protection and oversee the process, using the following invocation:

*'Archangel Auriel, help me to release my fears and phobias. Assist me in harmonizing the feminine, intuitive aspect of my being.'*

6 Place 12 of the moonstones evenly around your body, ensuring that one is directly above your head and one is beneath and between your feet. Put the thirteenth crystal on your Third Eye Chakra.

7 Take some slow, deep breaths in and out, making sure that the out-breath is slower than the in-breath.

8 Begin to focus on your emotions and, when you feel ready, ask the Archangel Auriel to send down the energies of the moon.

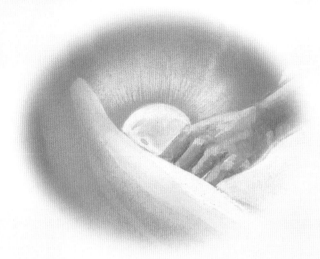

9 Imagine the moon energy descending: see it as a spiral of silvery light. Feel it flowing into your Crown Chakra and spiralling down through all your chakras in sequential order.

10 Feel every cell in your body being cleansed, purified and nurtured. Feel yourself, and your sense of purpose, being renewed.

11 Give yourself plenty of time to come back to everyday reality, by earthing and centring yourself (see page 76).

## INVOKE YOUR MOON ANGEL

Everyone has their own personal moon angel. This angel attended your birth to ensure that the moment when you took your first breath was in precise accordance with the needs of the higher self, for your soul's evolution. You can summon the Archangel Auriel to reconnect you with your moon angel, using the invocation given above.

# Archangel Camael

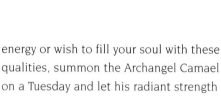

**His name means** He who sees God
**Colour** Orange
**Healing temple** Mars
**Crystal** Carnelian
**Tree of Life** Geburah
**How he helps** Heals the male aspect of your personality, overcoming anger and aggression and releasing pent-up emotions; offers justice and retribution

The Archangel Camael is often regarded as the commander-in-chief of the order of Powers. Camael is only one of various spellings of his name – Kamael, Khamael and Chamuel are also used.

The loving side of Camael's nature is shown when he helps you heal your relationships and find your soulmate. The warrior – the protector who helps you balance your male aspect – is the fierce Archangel Camael. As commander-in-chief of the Powers, he is also responsible for guarding the pathways that lead to Heaven, for keeping the world in balance and defending your soul against demonic attack. In addition, he has the power to punish and forgive, as well as to deliver a 'wake-up call'.

## SEEK JUSTICE

The Archangel Camael's day is Tuesday. Sometimes you have to stand firm for what you believe in, and this is not always easy, because it takes conviction, strength, endurance and stamina. If you believe that your cause is just and you need extra energy or wish to fill your soul with these qualities, summon the Archangel Camael on a Tuesday and let his radiant strength empower and reaffirm you.

To increase your power when you need justice in your personal battles, write a petition (letter) on a Tuesday, hold a carnelian crystal, and then place both petition and crystal on your angelic altar (see pages 42–43). After seven days burn your petition and remove the carnelian. Camael's energy is both swift and uncompromising, so you can expect to get results very quickly, but make sure that your call for justice is appropriate and in accordance with your own karmic lessons.

Carnelian is a crystal that helps you flow harmoniously with your own energy system and your surroundings. It brings flexibility in resolving conflicts caused by the need to assert yourself. In your struggle for self-determination, anger and aggression can sometimes lodge in your emotional or mental body and, if they are not released, they may turn into hostility and bitterness.

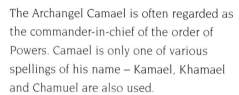

## CAMAEL AS THE ANGEL OF MARS

As the ruler of Mars, the Archangel Camael shares Mars' characteristics. Astrologically, Mars is seen as a planet of conflict, constantly at war with the other planets, and this negative aspect includes ruthlessness, brutality and wanton destruction. Mars' positive aspects are courage, passion, will power and the necessary skills to flourish amid the storm of chaos.

## MEDITATION TO RELEASE PENT-UP EMOTIONS

Healing the male aspect of your personality by displacing pent-up emotions, such as anger, rage and hostility, is the focus of this meditation. As the negative emotions are released, your body is filled with the positive male attributes of the Archangel Camael: courage, stamina and the peaceful resolution of conflict.

This meditation is in two parts and may initially appear complicated because you have to focus first on the Sacral Chakra and then move the energy you have created (the life-force) up your spiritual spine (the subtle energy channel that runs from the perineum to the top of your head) into the Third Eye Chakra (also known as the 'golden gate'), where it is transformed into the 'golden sun-disc' energy.

It is very important to have cleared any energy blockages by releasing your fears and phobias, using the Archangel Auriel's calling-down-the-moon technique (see pages 120–121), before you can fully move the energy of the Sacral Chakra to the Third Eye Chakra for alchemical transformation.

### WHAT TO DO

1 Sit in a comfortable meditation posture (see page 60).

2 Take three slow, deep breaths and instruct your body to relax.

3 Call on the Archangel Camael for protection and to oversee the process.

**4** Focus your attention on your Sacral Chakra (your pelvis) and ask the Archangel Camael to transform any stored anger, aggression or pent-up emotions into positive, life-affirming energy.

**5** With each in-breath, feel your Sacral Chakra filling with the life-force. As you inhale, breathe deeply, drawing the breath into your belly by expanding and pushing out the muscles, and as you exhale, pull in the lower abdomen. This is called abdominal breathing.

**6** Once you have built up this energy (it should feel like an inflated orange balloon), use the power of your intent (will) to let that energy spiral upwards to your Third Eye Chakra. Symbolically, the Third Eye Chakra is represented by two pure white lotus petals on each side of a pure white circle. This is where the mind looks directly at itself, through the magic mirror of the moon. The two petals represent male and female balance, the sun and moon discs in harmony.

**7** Keeping your intent focused on your Third Eye Chakra, become aware of the two energies that are now contained in this centre.

**8** See the lunar disc (silver) over your left eye and the solar disc (golden) over your right eye.

**9** Allow these two energies to harmonize and balance. As they do so, they transform into one disc, the colour of white gold, positioned right between your eyes.

**10** Stay with this harmonious energy as long as you like. To finish the meditation, allow the energy you have created to flow though all your subtle energy channels, purifying everything it touches.

**11** Give yourself plenty of time to come back to everyday reality, by earthing and centring yourself (see page 76).

# Archangel Seraphiel

**His name means** The inflamer of God
**Colour** Cosmic light
**Healing temple** Luxor, Egypt
**Crystal** Seriphos quartz
**Tree of Life** Kether
**How he helps** Awakens your true angelic nature; clears karmic and ancestral miasms (energy imprints)

The Archangel Seraphiel is sometimes called the Prince of Peace. He is the ruler of the Seraphim, the highest-ranking choir of angels, who are also known as the Angels of Light. They bring an awakening/healing energy known as 'brilliance'. This is pure cosmic iridescent light, which contains all the colours and 'rays' (including those invisible rays that the human eye cannot see). The Archangel Seraphiel (like the other Seraphim, whose essence is perfect love), directs the Divine energy that emanates from the first creative source.

'Seraph' means 'the inflamer', from the Hebraic word *saraph*, which translates as 'burning'. The Seraphim are the angels of Divine fire, and in the Bible they placed a glowing coal on Isaiah's lips to cleanse him. Seraphim have six wings: two cover their face, two cover their feet, and they use the other two to fly with.

If you call on the Seraphims' power, your being will be flooded with infinite love and light. And Enoch, a Hebrew prophet who named many of the Archangels, reported that the Archangel Seraphiel is the most brilliant of all the angelic beings. You cannot summon him at will, but you can petition him through quiet contemplation to assist you in finding inner peace. He is the highest-ranking prince of the Merkavah, the mystical way fo ascending through the Seven Heavens (see pages 146–149).

## MIASMS

Seraphiel's speciality is clearing 'miasms', or subtle energy imprints. You can think of a 'miasm' as a 'crystallized pattern' that lodges in any of the subtle body systems, causing illness. There are four basic types: karmic, acquired, ancestral and planetary.

- Karmic miasms are the residue of past-life actions that lodge in the etheric body and have the potential to develop into illness or suffering in the present or future lives. This often determines your attitude and behaviour.

- Acquired miasms are acute or infectious diseases or petrochemical toxicity acquired during this lifetime. After the acute phase of an illness, these miasmatic traits predispose you to other related illnesses.

- Ancestral miasms are passed down to you from your ancestors.

- Planetary miasms are stored in the collective consciousness of the planet at the etheric level. They may penetrate the physical body or the subtle bodies.

You can use the following invocation to clear certain miasms:

*'Archangel Seraphiel, assist me in releasing all karmic and ancestral miasms. I now allow angelic healing and peace to manifest in my life.'*

## ATTUNEMENT TO CLEANSE THE AURIC LAYERS

This exercise is simple but powerful, especially when performed for the first time. Some people are aware of the seven different layers of the aura (which begin with the physical body and progress through the emotions to more subtle, spiritual levels); they are also conscious of any energy that is not smooth and light. If you detect stagnant, prickly or heavy energy, let the subtle essence of the Archangel Seraphiel cleanse it. If you find any cords, hooks or attachments within your chakras or your aura, simply ask him to remove and transmute them.

The brilliance of the Archangel Seraphiel will then awaken you to the angelic domain. Be prepared to move forward spiritually when you work with the Seraphim, because they direct the radiant light of God, which has the power to modify all conditions that afflict the body, mind and spirit.

### WHAT TO DO

1 Ask the Archangel Seraphiel to send down a sphere of cosmic iridescent light. Feel it entering your Soul Star Chakra (one of the transcendental chakras, located about 15–17 cm/6–7 in above the top of the head; it activates your 'light body') and moving downwards into your Crown Chakra. As it does so, your whole being is flooded with light.

2 You should perform this attunement standing; you are going to use your hands to cleanse your aura. Begin by raising your hands above your head and

start to cleanse your aura, using gentle, sweeping movements. Start with the Crown Chakra, asking that it be blessed and filled with angelic light.

3 Move downwards through all your chakras in sequential order: Third Eye, Throat, Heart, Solar Plexus and Root. As you cleanse each chakra, ask for a blessing and protection to be placed over it.

4 Continue downwards, cleansing your legs and the area beneath your feet. Then cleanse the area you are standing on.

5 Touch the floor with the tips of your fingers and connect with the consciousness of the Earth. Ask for a blessing to be placed on your Earth connection.

6 Now stand up straight and raise your arms high above your head. Stretch your fingers upwards and, as you do so, feel angelic hands coming down to you: let the Seraphim place their hands in yours.

7 Ask for a blessing to be placed on your hands that will empower your angelic therapy work.

8 When you feel ready, let your angelic wings grow out of the space between your shoulder blades. Feel them growing upwards and outwards. Sense how they feel, what they look like: are they fluffy and covered in white feathers; are they gossamer, as light as air; or are they starlight?

9 Let your wings unfurl fully and allow your body to adjust to the experience of having wings. Often you will feel a shift in your overall energy field as your vibrational rate is raised and you grow accustomed to the experience.

10 See if you can move your wings to the rhythm of your heartbeat. Ask for a blessing to be placed on them, and let them help you 'fly' through life, raising you above the everyday cares and concerns of the human mind, which has in the past dulled your senses to the beauty of God all around you.

11 Close the session by thanking the Archangel Seraphiel for his help and blessings.

12 Give yourself plenty of time to come back to everyday reality, by earthing and centring yourself (see page 76).

# Archangel Tzaphkiel

**Her name means** Knowledge of God
**Colour** Lavender-blue
**Healing temple** Atlantic Ocean (where the ancient island civilization of Atlantis once flourished)
**Crystals** Tanzanite, amethyst
**Tree of Life** Binah
**How she helps** Assists in the contemplation of God, understanding, mindfulness

The Archangel Tzaphkiel (Zaphkiel) is the Archangel of deep contemplation of God, representing the Divine, feminine, watery aspect of creation. She has the power to nurture all things and give glimpses of other realities. Tzaphkiel will catch you if you fall or falter, for the feminine aspect of God's love is unconditional and non-judgemental. Allow her to carry you when you feel emotionally weak, for her infinite compassion is the sea of your liberation.

Tzaphkiel's healing energy takes you beyond the confines of the Earth plane into a space where you learn to nurture yourself by letting go of the past to find inner peace. Tzaphkiel is sometimes portrayed as the Great Mother, the Queen of the Stars or as the Divine spark 'trapped within each soul incarnate'.

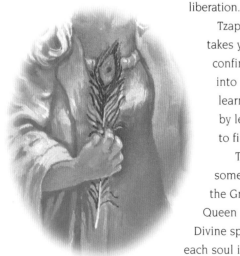

## USE CRYSTALS TO RECEIVE INSIGHTS

The Archangel Tzaphkiel, by her very nature, bestows blessings that are designed to increase understanding by imparting wisdom that enhances spiritual growth. She casts out all that is superficial to spiritual development. She also increases insight, mysticism and discernment by helping to develop fully the feminine side of your nature. However, she will do this only if you ask to be reborn into a new level of consciousness, which allows your heart to open fully and your soul's purity to be made manifest on Earth for the freedom and salvation of all.

To do this technique you require a tanzanite crystal and some amethysts. Tanzanite is trichroic – that is, it shows different colours when viewed along three different axes. One axis shows blue, another lavender and the third bronze. This colour change facilitates altered states of reality, allowing for radical shifts in consciousness. Because tanzanite raises

the vibratory signature of the user, it expands the personal mandala, allowing for 'downloads' of information from the Akashic records (see page 20). Tanzanite is then used for both inner and outer journeys. Your raised vibratory rate will cause you to see a thinning of the veil between the various planes of consciousness, allowing for clear communication with angels, ascended Masters, spirit guides and other enlightened beings from dimensions that are not usually available to your normal conscious awareness. With dedicated use, tanzanite facilitates deep meditation, astral journeys and materialization on other planes of existence.

Amethyst, like most violet crystals, is helpful in expanding your consciousness to become aware of higher dimensions. It brings a state of balance to any area that requires it. The colour violet is the gateway to the unseen, freeing the imagination and taking you beyond your current knowledge into the unknown and miraculous. It is used for deep healing work and is especially useful for creating a peaceful mind. Amethyst balances the nervous system, so it is good for very sensitive individuals. It quickly reduces restlessness, irritation and worry – bringing an indefinable sense of peace. It also speeds up emotional and physical recovery.

## YOU WILL NEED

- A tanzanite crystal (natural or tumble-polished)
- Eight amethyst crystals (natural single-terminated or tumble-polished)
- A yoga mat or pad

## WHAT TO DO

1 Cleanse your crystals before using them (see page 55).

2 Lie on the floor, using a yoga mat or pad to make yourself comfortable.

3 Ask the Archangel Tzaphkiel to oversee the process.

4 Place the amethyst crystals evenly spaced around your body, including one above your head and one beneath your feet. (If you have natural single-terminated crystals, place them so that they face inwards.)

5 Put the tanzanite crystal on your Third Eye Chakra.

6 Visualize the healing energy entering and filling your body.

7 The process is complete when you feel a change of emotion, or when you experience feelings of balance and inner peace. Use this technique often to nurture yourself and remove negative emotional patterns that have prevented you from moving forward.

# MEDITATION TO PROMOTE MINDFULNESS

Before you can begin the journey back to God, you need to clear your emotional and mental clutter to discover who you truly are. You need to let go of the past in order to move forwards. There are many distractions in life, and you are probably so busy that you sometimes lose yourself along the way. You forget the reality of your existence and your reason for leaving your cosmic mother and father and for incarnating in the first place. You need to learn discrimination and discernment. You also need to become aware of influences all around so that you can distinguish between what is good and what is bad.

Archangel Tzaphkiel is the 'Cosmic Mother' – the one who bestows understanding that will guide you. She rules over Binah, the third sphere of the revered trinity at the top of the Tree of Life. It is here that conception takes place when the seed of life enters from Kether (the Divine), passes through Chokmah (the Cosmic Father) and into Binah. This cosmic conception within the womb of Binah is, as *The Zohar* (see page 14) depicts, 'an explosion of light'. It is here that all other sparks of life are generated, which then flow outwards into all worlds and dimensions.

You should undertake the following technique gently, because if you try too hard you will not succeed.

## WHAT TO DO

1 Choose a time and place when you will not be disturbed – a time when you can be alone with your thoughts. Then allot a specific duration to this exercise (perhaps 10 minutes to begin with).

2 For the length of time that you do this exercise, just be aware of your thoughts. Do not let anything that happens prevent you from focusing on them.

3 What did you notice? Normally your thoughts jump about and you easily lose yourself. A thought enters your head or someone walks past, and immediately you are inside your head again, following that thought or person, and you lose yourself in the real world. After practising this technique a few times you may begin to notice the 'chattering monkey' that is your mind. If you keep practising it, you may find that your mind occasionally slows down. This will give you a glimpse of what reality really is, and what it could be like to live in the present moment – in mindfulness.

# Archangel Uriel

**His name means** Fire of God or Light of God
**Colour** Ruby-red through to deep purple
**Healing temple** Tatra Mountains, Poland
**Crystals** Ruby, magenta garnet
**Tree of Life** Malkuth
**How he helps** Illuminates your path and promotes peace

Uriel (Oriel) is one of the most powerful Archangels. He is the Angel of the Presence and is able to reflect the unimaginable light that is God. He is associated with electricity, lightning, thunder and sudden action, and is often depicted holding a scroll or carrying a staff.

He is the invincible angel of power, authority and Divine retribution. He is also a steadfast guide for humanity and may be called upon in moments of extreme crisis. He gives effective practical assistance and helps bring about a peaceful resolution of problems. This is why he is also known as the Angel of Peace.

The staff that Uriel carries represents your spinal column, which reflects on personal issues of support and feelings of not being supported by family, work, society and so on. The staff symbolically represents structure and balance and your ability to live harmoniously on the planet. If your spinal column is not balanced and all the chakra centres embedded in it – the 'I AM' column (your spiritual spine) – are not functioning harmoniously, you will not be able to support yourself.

## PEACE AND TRANQUILLITY

Call on the Archangel Uriel:

- If you are restless and feel incapable of inner stillness and peace.

- If your heart is troubled and your soul is in turmoil.

- If you need a peaceful resolution to problems.

- If you are full of painful emotions.

- If you need immediate practical assistance in times of crisis or danger.

- If you require support in overcoming self-destructive or suicidal feelings.

- If you wish to resolve global problems and bring world peace.

- If you are proud, impulsive, rash or boastful.

- If you feel separate from your own source of courage and power.

- If you feel insecure, apprehensive, distrustful or timid.

- If you need inner strength and self-assurance.

## ILLUMINATION

Summon the Archangel Uriel:

- To illuminate your path through life.

- To discover your reason for incarnating.

- To achieve your goals in life by making your dreams a reality.

- To become less self-centred and more in tune with the needs of others who are less fortunate than yourself.

- To open yourself to the infinite possibilities that are you.

- To manifest innovative new ideas and concepts.

- To ground and clarify spiritual experiences.

## FIATS TO THE ARCHANGEL URIEL

- Archangel Uriel, fill my life with peace and tranquillity.

- Archangel Uriel, illuminate my path through life.

- Archangel Uriel, bring world peace.

## DECREE TO THE ARCHANGEL URIEL

I AM infinite peace made manifest.

## CRYSTALS TO RELEASE THE SOUL'S POTENTIAL

Often people learn limiting emotional patterns in early childhood and, if these are not released, you will not feel fulfilled, whole and successful. This crystal technique will release your soul's true potential, improving your self-confidence and your relationships with others.

### YOU WILL NEED
- Seven rubies (tumble-polished)
- A yoga mat or pad

### WHAT TO DO

1 Cleanse your crystals before using them (see page 55).

2 Lie on the floor, using a yoga mat or pad to make yourself comfortable.

3 Invoke the Archangel Uriel to oversee the process.

4 Place six of the tumbled rubies evenly around your body: one directly above your head, one beneath and between your feet, and one level with each knee and elbow. Place the seventh ruby on your Heart Chakra.

5 Visualize the healing energy entering and filling your body.

6 Begin with a short session of five minutes.

7 Give yourself plenty of time to come back to everyday reality, by earthing and centring yourself (see page 76).

# TEMPLE MEDITATION

This meditation will clarify your reasons for incarnating in this lifetime.

## WHAT TO DO

1 Sit comfortably, close your eyes and focus on your Heart Chakra.

2 Summon the Archangel Uriel, using the following invocation:

*'Archangel Uriel, bring peace to my troubled mind and spirit. Reveal to me that which is true. Dissolve all obstacles on my spiritual path. Resolve all my hidden issues. Cleanse my body and mind to allow the power of peace to flow through me. Make me a pure channel of God's infinite peace. Show me my true path in life so that I can fulfil my Dharma.'*

3 Let yourself be enveloped in the power and energy of the Archangel Uriel for as long as you like; when you are ready, allow yourself to be raised upwards on a spiral of ruby-violet light.

4 Slowly this light spiral raises you higher and higher. You feel yourself held safely in angelic arms and let yourself be transported gently to the Temple of Light.

5 You will be guided along sparkling crystalline corridors until you reach the Room of Peace, where you see a circle of ruby crystal light in front of you. In the centre of this is a white lotus flower, and in the centre of the lotus is a beautiful, faceted ruby pulsating with the life-force.

6 A vision arises from the lotus flower: it is a tree, and around it are wound the coils of unsubstantiated desire and illusion that you have allowed to coil around your heart. These coils are bound very tightly and stop you finding inner peace and blossoming into the infinite being of love and light that you truly are. You instinctively know these coils must be released. Your heart energy must be freed, and you must expand your being. As you watch the vision, you see the coils begin to loosen and fall away; you see the tree burst into a golden flame; as you gaze a little longer, you see that it is blossoming, ready to bear fruit.

7 Now you are approached by the Archangel Uriel. You are asked if you wish to visit the Scroll Room, where billions of scrolls are stored – one for each person incarnate on the planet. Your own scroll is here in this room and contains your Dharma: your soul agreement, your 'gift' to humanity. This represents your true path in life. If you choose to see your scroll, it will be handed to you with great reverence. It is up to you whether you choose to open and read it. Whatever happens, simply allow the process to unfold.

8 The Archangel Uriel will let you know when it is time to leave and will bring you safely back into your body, to the here and now.

9 Give yourself plenty of time to come back to everyday reality, by earthing and centring yourself (see page 76).

# Archangel Gabriel

**His name means** God is my strength
**Colour** Shining white
**Healing temple** Mount Shasta, California, USA
**Crystal** Danburite
**Tree of Life** Yesod
**How he helps** Offers guidance, spiritual awakening, purification, inspiration and dream interpretation

The Archangel Gabriel, the messenger, is one of only two angels mentioned by name in the Old Testament (the other being the Archangel Michael). Muslims say that Gabriel (Jibril) awakened the prophet of God, Muhammad, and dictated the Koran (the sacred book of Islam) to him. Gabriel is well known in Christianity too: he announced the forthcoming birth of Jesus, the Christ child, to his mother Mary, and was there at Jesus' death as the angel who watched over the tomb and gave the good news of his resurrection to the disciples (although he is

not specifically mentioned by name). It is said that Joan of Arc was also inspired by the Archangel Gabriel.

Gabriel's planet is the moon, and he is sometimes known as the Angel of the Moon. He uses this feminine, intuitive energy to help you interpret dreams and visions, and employs the moon's magical energy to awaken humanity. He is often depicted carrying a golden trumpet, which he uses to awaken your inner angel and bring good news. He is the Archangel who guides you through life-changing experiences, and he will dissolve your fear through his cleansing white ray of purification.

You can summon the Archangel Gabriel and ask for his guidance when you are undertaking a new project, considering a career change or even thinking of starting a family. Seek him out to help you through life-changing events; ask him to guide you at night while you sleep and to help you pay attention to your inner world; ask him to be your muse and to alert you to the angelic coincidences in your life.

## VISUALIZATION TO SUMMON ANGELIC GUIDES

You can ask the Archangel Gabriel to send you angelic guides to help you in a particular situation.

### WHAT TO DO

1 Sit in a comfortable meditation posture (see page 60).

2 Ask the Archangel Gabriel to protect you and oversee this process.

3 Take some slow, deep breaths in and out, making the out-breath slower than the in-breath.

4 Systematically relax all of your body: start at your feet and work upwards until you reach your head.

5 Visualize the life situation on which you are seeking guidance: see it surrounded by pure white light.

6 Let the pure white light transform into angelic guides – see yourself supported by these angels. Be aware of any changes that you feel in your body, especially in your Heart Chakra.

7 Give yourself plenty of time to come back to everyday reality, by earthing and centring yourself (see page 76).

## FIATS TO THE ARCHANGEL GABRIEL

- Archangel Gabriel, reveal to me my soul's purpose.

- Archangel Gabriel, inspire and uplift me.

- Archangel Gabriel, assist me in understanding my dreams.

- Archangel Gabriel, clarify my visions and help me develop my inner sight.

- Archangel Gabriel, show me my soul's true potential.

- Archangel Gabriel, take me in my soul consciousness to your etheric temple.

## PURIFICATION

Call on the Archangel Gabriel:

- To help you clear your clutter and thereby bring order and discipline to your life.

- To cleanse toxins from your body and help you initiate a healthy eating regime.

- To purify your emotional and mental baggage.

- To purify your home after you have been robbed.

- To cleanse your body and emotions if you have been assaulted in any way.

- To purify you and your environment if you are being psychically attacked.

# CRYSTAL TECHNIQUE FOR PURIFICATION

This exercise shows you how to make a purification essence, which you can take internally or use in a body spray, bath or massage oil. It uses danburite, a crystal that cleanses toxins from all levels of the body and from the aura (for additional properties, see page 57).

## YOU WILL NEED

- A clear glass or quartz crystal bowl
- A large amber-coloured glass bottle
- An amber-coloured glass dropper bottle
- A danburite crystal (natural or tumble-polished)
- A clear quartz crystal (natural or tumble-polished) to amplify the energies of the danburite
- Distilled water
- Brandy

## WHAT TO DO

1 Sterilize the glass bowl and the bottles (you can buy sterilizing equipment from most pharmacies).

2 Cleanse your crystals before using them (see page 55).

3 Place the crystals in the bowl and cover them with distilled water.

4 Position the bowl so that it will be in direct early-morning sunlight on a day when there are no clouds. Always bring the bowl inside before noon, when the sun's energy changes and becomes energetically draining. Two to three hours in full sunlight should be sufficient to imprint the subtle energy of the minerals into the water.

5 Fill one-third of your mother bottle with the solution and make up the remaining two-thirds with brandy.

6 Put seven drops from the mother bottle into the dropper bottle. Then add one-third brandy and two-thirds distilled water; alternatively, add just water, in which case the dropper bottle must be kept in a refrigerator and the solution will last for only one week.

7 Label the dropper bottle with the name of the crystals, the date made and the number and frequency of drops required. Normally seven drops are taken three times a day, although the essence may be taken as often as necessary.

8 To use the purification essence, place up to seven drops from the dropper bottle directly under the tongue; put seven drops in a small glass of mineral water and sip slowly throughout the day; place seven drops in an atomizer bottle filled with distilled water, then spray around your body as often as required; or add a few drops to your bath water or to a massage oil.

# Archangel Zadkiel

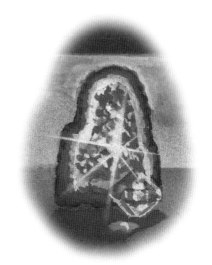

**His name means** Righteousness of God
**Colour** Violet
**Healing temple** Cuba
**Crystals** Amethyst, moldavite
**Tree of Life** Chesed
**How he helps** Promotes self-transformation, freedom, spiritual growth, joy and cosmic alchemy

The Archangel Zadkiel (Tzadkiel) is the angel of mercy, who teaches trust in God and the benevolence of God. He brings comfort in your hour of need. He is the regent of Jupiter and of Thursday. Zadkiel is often portrayed holding a dagger, because he stopped Abraham from sacrificing his son Isaac on Mount Moriah. He is the leader of the angelic order of dominions and one of the seven Archangels who stand before the throne of God.

Zadkiel is also the guardian of the 'violet flame' – a spiritual energy that transforms lower energies into positive life-affirming energy. It is used for spiritual growth, self-transformation, joy and emotional freedom. Violet represents a balance of blue and red. As Sir Isaac Newton discovered, translucent violet is the ray which has the shortest wavelength. It also has the fastest vibration in the rainbow and, as such, symbolizes a point of transition between what is visible and invisible to normal human vision. It has always represented Divine alchemy and the transmutation of energy from gross physical form into the unmanifested Divine.

## INVOKE THE VIOLET FLAME OF COSMIC FREEDOM

- To cleanse all areas of your mind, body and emotions.

- To instantly purify all your chakras and your aura.

- To bring relief from addictions and addictive traits within your personality.

- To amplify other healing and spiritual energies.

- To awaken the Divine spark within you, thus aiding your spiritual growth.

- To calm your mind before meditation or to ease insomnia and nightmares.

Use the following invocation:

*'Archangel Zadkiel, cleanse me with your violet flame of cosmic freedom and joy.'*

## VISUALIZATION TO CREATE LIFE-AFFIRMING ENERGY

Remember how, when you were a child, every harsh word or criticism (no matter how well meant) wounded your heart. Negative memories can be one of the most difficult things to overcome and release and can subtly affect the way you relate to other people and the way you view yourself. These memories may be hidden in your subconscious mind and can leave you open to all kinds of negative behaviour. By invoking the violet flame of the Archangel Zadkiel you can change this negative energy into positive, life-affirming energy, in a process known as 'transmutation'.

### WHAT TO DO

1 Sit comfortably in a chair.

2 Start by visualizing roots growing from the soles of each foot – extend them deep into the earth. This will establish a strong connection to the earth, making you feel safe, balanced and receptive.

3 Begin to relax each part of your body, starting at your feet and legs and working systematically through the whole of your body, right up to the top of your head.

4 Release any remaining tension by scanning your body from the top of your head to the tips of your toes. If you feel any tension, tighten the muscles in that area and, as you relax them, breathe out to release the tension.

5 Summon the Archangel Zadkiel and ask him to oversee the process. You could use his invocation (see page 142) or the following decree: 'I AM a being of violet flame.' Visualize yourself completely surrounded and engulfed by this violet flame.

6 Begin to let any negative memories that you wish to release come to the surface of your conscious mind, ready for transmutation. Some people think through their life year by year, starting at the moment of conception; others focus first on their most painful memory.

7 The session is concluded once the violet flame has diminished.

8 Affirm that from now on you will treat everyone you meet with compassion and will understand that, like you, they are going through the learning experience called life. Resolve to be forgiving of others and to learn to forgive yourself.

# CRYSTAL TECHNIQUE TO DEVELOP YOUR CROWN CHAKRA

The Archangel Zadkiel's speciality is helping you to develop (evolve) your Crown Chakra by freeing your mind of all limitations. The Crown Chakra is related to openness: if you get over-attached to a closed way of thinking or feeling, this prevents you from developing compassion and being able to consider all possibilities. Zadkiel encourages you to free yourself from emotional attachments, which enables you to achieve your spiritual goals. The Crown Chakra is symbolically represented as a thousand-petalled white lotus flower.

At some stage when you work with the Archangel Zadkiel, he will aid you in resolving contradictions. This releases an amazing amount of pent-up energy (life-force), which you can then use to move on to the next level of your spiritual development – cosmic consciousness. Zadkiel resolves conflicts by teaching you to perceive many different things at the same time, or many different points of view. This in turn shows you how seemingly irreconcilable ideas can be united in perfect harmony.

This exercise uses moldavite, a transformational stone from the stars; it is a tektite (believed to be a product of meteoric impact) that came to Earth more than 15 million years ago. Moldavite is amorphous, meaning that it has no crystalline structure, so it can take you into uncharted realms of infinite possibilities – cosmic alchemy.

## YOU WILL NEED

- Two amethysts (natural single-terminated)
- Two moldavite tektites (natural or faceted)
- A yoga mat or pad

## WHAT TO DO

1 Cleanse your crystals before using them (see page 55).

2 Lie on the floor, using a yoga mat or pad to make yourself comfortable.

3 Invoke the Archangel Zadkiel to oversee this powerful process, which will expand your awareness.

4 Place an amethyst on each side of your head, level with the top of your ears and with the terminations pointing outwards.

5 Place the moldavite tektites as follows: one on your Third Eye Chakra and one slightly above your Crown Chakra.

6 Visualize the healing energy entering and filling your body.

7 You should not stay in this energy for longer than ten minutes at a time.

8 Give yourself plenty of time to come back to everyday reality, by earthing and centring yourself (see page 76).

9 Write down your impressions and experiences in your angel journal (see page 41).

# Archangel Melchizedek

**His name means** King of peace and righteousness
**Colour** White-gold
**Healing temple** Jerusalem
**Crystal** Rutile quartz
**Tree of Life** Kether
**How he helps** Aids spiritual growth, rainbow healing and the mystical journey through the labyrinth of life

The Archangel Melchizedek is also known as Lord Melchizedek or Melchisedec. He took human form as a priest and king of Salem (present-day Jerusalem) to form the order of Melchizedek and coordinate the work of the Christ energy on Earth.

In the New Testament (Hebrews 6:20) it states that 'Jesus has gone as a forerunner on our behalf, having become a high priest forever in the order of Melchizedek'. Melchizedek is also called the king of peace and righteousness, and Hebrews 7:3 states, 'He was without father or mother or genealogy, and has neither beginning of days nor end of life, but resembling the Son of God he continues a priest forever.'

Traditional Jewish angelology holds the belief that the divide between human and angelic form is not fixed, but that perfected humans – those who reach the highest spiritual level – can become angels.

## THE MERKAVAH

In ancient times the Merkavah or Merkaba mystics (*merkavah* is a Hebrew word for chariot) imagined the throne of God as a throne with wheels. The ancient *Hekhaloth* (Jewish texts), and the mystic who compiled them in the 5th and 6th centuries CE, were inspired by the angels of the chariot throne. Nobody knows the exact date of the writings, but the images in these texts are extracted from temple worship in the Holy of Holies (the most sacred place). Some of the texts describe personal preparation using purification and prayer, and how a person could ascend to stand before the throne.

Once a mystic stands before the throne of God, he is taught the heart of creation (how the Merkavah works) and then brings this knowledge back to Earth to teach to his students. Jesus was the greatest Merkavah mystic, and when he was baptized he saw the heavens open and heard that he was the Son of God. The Bible goes on to describe how Jesus was tested in the desert, and his ascent is

described in The Book of Revelation. He received the scroll of knowledge because he was worthy, and he would be enthroned above all angels.

The way of the Merkavah mystic requires a profound illumination of the mind and heart. Both must be pierced by light. The aura that encircles them must become like a wheel of flame. The chakras, the seven great circular seals embedded within your spiritual spine, must be aflame with the light of God.

Just as your angelic guardian beholds the face of God in Heaven, so you must hold the presence of God on the Earthly plane by becoming aware of the Divine spark that resides within your Heart Chakra. More importantly, you must let it guide you daily.

The Archangel Melchizedek and his order transmit to humanity the Keys to the Kingdom. These keys are encoded in transmissions of light frequencies, which penetrate the human body. Those who receive them and apply them become the Family of Light by awakening their 'Merkavah body'. The mass awakening of humanity to the presence of angels has been prophesied – and angels will once again walk the Earth with their human companions.

If you believe that angels are not just beautiful figments of humans' imagination or the stuff of myth and legend, and that you too could become an angel, then the Archangel Melchizedek is the angel to summon.

## CHAKRAS AND RAYS

| Chakra | Transmuting ray | Properties |
| --- | --- | --- |
| Root | White | Purification, resurrection |
| Sacral | Violet | Freedom, forgiveness |
| Solar Plexus | Ruby | Devotion, peace |
| Heart | Pink | Adoration, Divine love |
| Throat | Indigo | Mystery, miracles |
| Third Eye | Emerald-green | Divine vision |
| Crown | White-gold | Illumination, wisdom |

# USE CRYSTALS TO AWAKEN THE MERKAVAH BODY

In the section on the Angels of the Rays (see pages 48–50) you saw how seven Archangels direct the vital life-force of God to develop the chakra system. In this section you begin to develop your chakra centres and shift your awareness and to become more spiritually aware. As you evolve spiritually, so your physical body and your third-dimensional chakra system and frequency also evolve. This causes a thinning of the 'veil' between dimensions. To become aware of the higher dimensions and activate your Merkavah vehicle, you can use this exercise to call down the transmuting rays of the fourth-dimensional chakra system (see below). The Archangel Melchizedek is the angel who assists you and oversees this process.

## YOU WILL NEED
- 12 rutile quartz crystals (tumble-polished)
- A yoga mat or pad

## WHAT TO DO

1 Cleanse your crystals before using them (see page 55).

2 Lie on the floor, using a yoga mat or pad to make yourself comfortable.

3 Invoke the Archangel Melchizedek to guide, protect and oversee the process.

4 Place the rutile quartz crystals evenly around your body, with one directly above your head and one directly beneath and between your feet.

5 Ask the Archangel Melchizedek to send down the fourth-dimensional chakra rays. He will send them down starting from the Root Chakra and working up to the Crown Chakra. As each ray descends, you will feel it transmuting the chakra centre to which it relates.

6 When you have finished the process, concentrate on breathing in the white-gold light of the Archangel Melchizedek to cleanse, harmonize and integrate all your subtle energy channels – your own personal labyrinth. The practice of circulating the white-gold light of Melchizedek increases your internal light (your spiritual illumination), leading to enhanced sensitivity and an awareness that is mystical in nature.

7 Give yourself plenty of time to come back to everyday reality, by earthing and centring yourself (see page 76).

# Archangel Raziel

**His name means** Secret of God
**Colour** Indigo
**Healing temple** Pacific Ocean (where the lost land of Lemuria or Mu once flourished some 70,000 years ago)
**Crystal** Iolite
**Tree of Life** Chokmah
**How he helps** Imparts the secret mysteries of the universe and the gifts of clairvoyance, prophecy and revelation

Raziel (Ratziel) is the Archangel of the secret mysteries, who gives Divine information by allowing you to glimpse the enigma that is God. The experience of this Archangel takes your consciousness beyond the confines of time, so any glimpses of this level of existence will show past, present and future as the eternal now.

This experience is bestowed as knowledge and is total, absolute, unequivocal and perfect. When you receive these amazing insights, you need no confirmation of your understanding from others. Your Crown Chakra is opened, the flames of enlightenment descend, you transcend normal reality – you just *are*. In this eternal moment you experience your own immortality and Divinity; you literally gaze upon the 'countenance of God'. These encounters with Raziel can seem extreme to your friends, family, work colleagues and society in general, but once you have sure and certain knowledge of the workings of the Divine, nothing in your life will ever be the same again.

On the Kabalistic Tree of Life, the Archangel Raziel is the Cosmic Father or *Abba*, who rules over Chokmah, which is the second sphere of the trinity at the top of the Tree. The seed of life enters from Kether (the Divine), passes through Chokmah (the Cosmic Father) and into Binah (the Cosmic Mother). As the Cosmic Father, Raziel is the chief angel of the supreme mysteries (including the legendary book of Raziel, which holds all terrestrial and heavenly knowledge). This secret knowledge was bestowed on King Solomon, giving him the celestial wisdom that enabled him to build his temple using kabalistic lore.

The prophets Moses, Enoch and Noah, and the first man Adam, also benefited from encounters with Raziel. Noah was given the information he needed to build the Ark and rebuild the world after the great flood. According to sacred lore, the Archangel Raziel stands daily on Mount Horeb, proclaiming the secrets of human beings to all humankind.

# THE POWER OF TRANSCENDENCE

The secret mysteries of Raziel are not for everyone, for they take the recipient into the heavenly realm where science and mysticism are the same – the quantum universe. If you feel a deep connection with the Archangel Raziel and you are drawn to working selflessly with sincere humility for the benefit and service of all, then summon this mysterious angel, because you will experience a metamorphosis. In fact, your life and the way you view the world will never be the same again.

These 'mind-blowing' encounters with the Archangel Raziel need some time to integrate fully with all levels of your being, or you could find yourself completely unbalanced. Such full-blown encounters usually occur only after many years of meditation, prayer, purification and total dedication to leading a spiritual life. Once this knowledge has been assimilated, most people who receive Raziel's transcendence become teachers and writers, sharing their abundance, wisdom and understanding with the world. Raziel awakens the prophets and religious reformers, so use the power wisely and become a father to all.

The ray through which the Archangel Raziel works is indigo, which is a perfect balance of dark blue and dark violet. Indigo aids intuition and spiritual knowledge. It is the strongest painkiller of the rainbow spectrum and can release negativity from the skeletal structure. It is also an astral antiseptic, which transmutes and purifies negativity. Indigo is good for spiritual teachers and writers, instilling in them humility, mercy and wisdom. This colour can be addictive, though, as it holds the domain of mystery, miracles and psychic understanding.

## TIPS

*Absorbing this experience is difficult, but the following steps will help you to integrate the impressions.*

- *Thinking about your experience brings it into the mental body – the Solar Plexus Chakra.*

- *Turning your experience into images brings it into the emotional body – the Heart Chakra.*

- *Talking about your experience with another person anchors it in the physical body via the Throat Chakra.*

- *Writing down your experiences for future reference (including the drawing of images) anchors it in the Sacral and Root Chakras.*

*Each step takes time and takes you a little further from the actual experience, but a lot of genuine clairvoyance ends up as illusion if it is not fully grounded in the physical realm.*

## CRYSTAL TECHNIQUE GIVING INSIGHT INTO THE SECRET MYSTERIES

This is a powerful process that develops your sensitivity, intuition, prophetic abilities and clairvoyance. It uses iolite, the stone of prophecy and vision. Iolite promotes full psychic activation and integration, but only if the five lower chakras are fully balanced; otherwise there is a danger of over-stimulation, which can bring disorientation.

### YOU WILL NEED

- Four iolite crystals (natural or tumble-polished)
- A yoga mat or pad

### WHAT TO DO

1 Cleanse your crystals before using them (see page 55).

2 Lie on the floor, using a yoga mat or pad to make yourself comfortable.

3 Call upon the Archangel Raziel to guide, protect and oversee the process, using the following invocation:

*'Archangel Raziel, grant me mercy by allowing my sins to be cleansed in the purification of your lightning flash. Restore the Divine blueprint, not only of my soul but of all creation, so that all souls are restored to their original perfect design. In the dark night when my soul is sorely tested, send your light to illuminate my path so that I can ascend swiftly to your Divine grace. Hallelujah.'*

4 Place three of the iolite crystals in a triangle around your body: one above your head and two beneath and to the sides of your feet.

5 Put the fourth iolite crystal on your Third Eye Chakra.

6 Visualize the healing energy entering and filling your body.

7 Because this is a powerful technique, you should not stay in this energy for more than 20 minutes at a time.

8 Give yourself plenty of time to come back to everyday reality, by earthing and centring yourself (see page 76).

9 Write down your impressions and experiences in your angel journal (see page 41).

# Archangel Metatron

**His name means** Angel of the Presence
**Colour** Brilliant white
**Healing temple** Luxor, Egypt
**Crystal** Diamond
**Tree of Life** Kether
**How he helps** Aids spiritual evolution, enlightenment, light-body activation and ascension into higher states of awareness and bliss

The Archangel Metatron brings unprecedented spiritual growth. He *is* the 'angel of ascension'. He is also known as the Prince of the Angels and as guardian of the threshold. Behind him stands the void; below him are all the other Archangels. The void contains all possibilities and, when you traverse this 'space', you come face to face with the Godhead. This is the ultimate goal of human existence; it is the place where all religions are one, all knowledge is one, all consciousness is one.

On your path 'home' to the stillness of the 'one heart', Metatron is your most important guide in the initiation process. As 'keeper of the Akashic records' (see page 20) – from which all individual sparks of consciousness arise – he holds the keys to understanding sacred geometry (metatronic sciences). He is said to have taken human form as the patriarch Enoch: he who 'walked with God and was not'. Once a human being has passed this level of consciousness, he cannot remain in a human body, hence the words 'was not'. Enoch was consumed by the luminous presence of God until his body was totally destroyed and he was pure spirit.

The Archangel Metatron is known as the guardian of the Tree of Life and as the Angel of the Presence. His vortex of light is so luminous and vast that you will often perceive him as a pillar of fire more dazzling than the sun. He is the light that Moses saw as the burning bush; he is the light that St Paul encountered on the road to Damascus. In fact, he is the light often seen by those who have undergone life-changing 'near-death experiences'.

## ALPHA AND OMEGA

Metatron is considered a vast angel. With Archangel Sandalphon (see pages 94–97), he represents the twin reflection of the Divine. As twins, they are the Alpha and Omega, the beginning and the end: their presence recalls the esoteric expression 'As above, so below'. On the Kabalistic Tree of Life, Metatron is in Kether, the Crown, representing the highest energy of the Divine. Kether is eternal: it has no beginning as it contains the Divine presence.

Working with the Archangel Metatron causes a download of information and understanding of the energy we call God. This is not a passive understanding of God but an active, dynamic flow of information. Metatronic energy carries with it great power, authority and responsibility. It allows access keys to 'star gates' (multiple inner dimensions and realities); it opens doors of communication with the highest vibrational beings. Working with Metatron greatly magnifies and hastens the process whereby those things that you hold in thought are brought into manifestation. Therefore you are advised to hold the highest thoughts while communing with his energies, in order to manifest that which will best serve both the individual and humanity.

## USE A CRYSTAL TO ACTIVATE THE LIGHT BODY

This is a powerful exercise to activate your 'light body', bringing spiritual evolution, ascension into higher states of awareness and enlightenment. It uses a diamond, whose brilliance and hardness make it the world's most valuable gemstone.

A diamond amplifies the energy of all other crystals. It is the ultimate enlightenment stone – indeed, it exemplifies the supreme ray of brilliance; it is pure, incorruptible, iridescent light. It contains all rays and brings them into perfect harmony: as such, it is a 'cure-all'. It has the power to pierce through negativity, bringing hope, beauty, light and healing. The diamond's energy is not earthly, but cosmic, responding to the universal mind from which all energy springs. A diamond adds lustre and beauty to everything it touches, but it will also show you your flaws; it is the hard, bright light that exposes all corruption, shams and evil. Its energy is very intense.

A diamond works especially well on the aura, dispelling any darkness that shrouds your light. Consciously holding a diamond in meditation and attuning to its energies enables you to 'see' the cleansing effect on the aura within seconds.

### YOU WILL NEED
- A diamond (natural or faceted)
- 12 clear quartz crystals (natural single-terminated)
- A yoga mat or pad

## WHAT TO DO

1 Cleanse your crystals before using them (see page 55).

2 Lie on the floor, using a yoga mat or pad to make yourself comfortable.

3 Ask the Archangel Metatron to guide, protect and oversee the process, saying the following:

*'Archangel Metatron, Angel of the Presence and all-seeing one, transform me with the sacred fire of the phoenix, so that I can rise from the ashes of my former illusory self. As the veils of ignorance and separation are removed from my eyes, may I become worthy of my crown of glory and unite my sacred I AM presence with I AM THAT I AM, so that I can shine like a diadem of beauty in the hand of God. Seal me with your perfect light. Guide me so that I can fulfil my soul's mission to allow the light of God to shine through me, to fill the Earth with Divine light so that peace can descend on Earth.'*

4 Place the quartz crystals evenly around your body, ensuring that one is directly above your head and one is directly beneath and between your feet, with the terminations pointing outwards.

5 Place the diamond on your Third Eye Chakra.

6 Visualize the healing energy entering and filling your body.

7 Because this is a powerful process, you should not stay in this energy for more than ten minutes at a time.

8 Give yourself plenty of time to come back to everyday reality, by earthing and centring yourself (see page 76).

9 Write down your impressions and experiences in your angel journal (see page 41).

### TIP

*It would also be beneficial to make a purification essence (see page 141 for instructions) or aura spray using a diamond. Take this essence daily to activate your 'light body'.*

# Index

# Acknowledgements

**Executive Editor** Sandra Rigby
**Managing Editor** Clare Churly
**Executive Art Editor** Sally Bond
**Designer** Martin Lovelock
**Illustrator** Stephen Angel
**Production Controller** Simone Nauerth